60* More Quick Baby Blankets

COZY KNITS IN THE
128 SUPERWASH & 220 SUPERWASH®
COLLECTIONS FROM CASCADE YARNS®

THE EDITORS OF SIXTH&SPRING BOOKS

sixth&springbooks NEW YORK

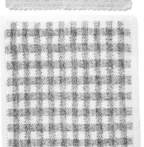

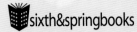

sixth&springbooks

104 W 27th St, 3rd Floor, New York, NY 10001
www.sixthandspring.com

Editor
CAROL J. SULCOSKI

Associate Editor
JACOB SEIFERT

Art Director
JOE VIOR

Yarn Editors
MATTHEW SCHRANK
JACLENE SINI

Supervising Patterns
Editor
CARLA SCOTT

Patterns Editors
LISA BUCCELLATO
THERESE CHYNOWETH
ROSEMARY DRYSDALE
RENEE LORION

Technical Illustrator
LORETTA DACHMAN

Photography
JACK DEUTSCH

Vice President/
Editorial Director
TRISHA MALCOLM

Vice President/
Publisher
CAROLINE KILMER

Production Manager
DAVID JOINNIDES

President
ART JOINNIDES

Chairman
JAY STEIN

Library of Congress Cataloging-in-Publication Data

Names: Cascade Yarns. | Sixth & Spring Books.
Title: 60 more quick baby blankets : cozy knits in the 128 Superwash and 220 Superwash collections from Cascade yarns / by the editors of Sixth&Spring Books.
Other titles: Sixty more quick baby blankets
Description: First edition. | New York : Sixth&Spring Books, 2017. | Includes index.
Identifiers: LCCN 2017002467 | ISBN 9781942021896 (pbk.)
Subjects: LCSH: Knitting—Patterns. | Blankets. | Infants' supplies.
Classification: LCC TT825.A1247 2017 | DDC 746.43/2—dc23
LC record available at https://lccn.loc.gov/2017002467

Manufactured in China

1 3 5 7 9 10 8 6 4 2

First Edition

contents

Nestle Your Wee Ones in Love—and Wool

Nothing gets the knitting mojo going like a new baby. And when you see this spectacular collection of blankets from the best-selling 60 Quick Knits series, you'll find plenty of stitching inspiration.

We've included projects for knitters of all skill levels, including beginners, and selected a wide range of styles: modular knits with squares and triangles, slip-stitch patterns that create intricate motifs, geometric designs with zigzags and diamonds, even a watermelon-inspired design and a bear-shaped snuggly. All designs are knit with the soft, durable, and easy-care 128 Superwash and 220 Superwash® collections from Cascade Yarns®, ensuring that your labor of love will be loved for many years to come.

To locate retailers that carry the 128 Superwash and 220 Superwash® collections from Cascade Yarns, visit cascadeyarns.com.

5

1

Head in the Clouds

Happy puffy clouds skitter across a blue sky,
ensuring that baby has a sunshiny day.

DESIGNED BY MELISSA DEHNCKE MCGILL

Knitted Measurements
Approx 24 x 32"/61 x 81cm

Materials
- 3 3½oz/100g hanks (each approx 220yd/200m) of Cascade Yarns *220 Superwash Effects* (superwash wool) in #3 Denim (A)
- 2 3½oz/100g balls (each approx 220yd/200m) of Cascade Yarns *220 Superwash* (superwash wool) in #871 White (B)
- One size 6 (4mm) circular needle, 32"/81cm long, *or size to obtain gauge*
- Stitch markers
- Bobbins

Seed Stitch
(over a multiple of 2 sts)
Row 1 *K1, p1; rep from * to end.
Row 2 P the knit sts and k the purl sts.
Rep row 2 for seed st.

Notes
1) Use a separate bobbin for each color section. Do *not* carry yarn across back of work. Twist yarns on WS to prevent holes in work.
2) Circular needle is used to accommodate large number of sts. Do *not* join.

Blanket
BOTTOM BORDER
With A, cast on 132 sts. Work 6 rows in seed st.

BEGIN CHART
Row 1 (RS) Work 6 sts in seed st as established for border, pm; *join bobbins of A and B as needed and work 40-st rep of chart, pm; rep from * twice more, pm; work 6 sts in seed st as established for border.
Cont in this manner, with first and last 6 sts in seed st, until 78 rows of chart have been worked 3 times.

TOP BORDER
Work all sts in A and seed st for 6 rows, removing markers on first row.
Bind off in pat.

Finishing
Weave in ends.
Block to measurements. ■

Gauge
22 sts and 30 rows to 4"/10cm over St st using size 6 (4mm) needle.
Take time to check gauge

1
Head in the Clouds

COLOR KEY

- A
- B

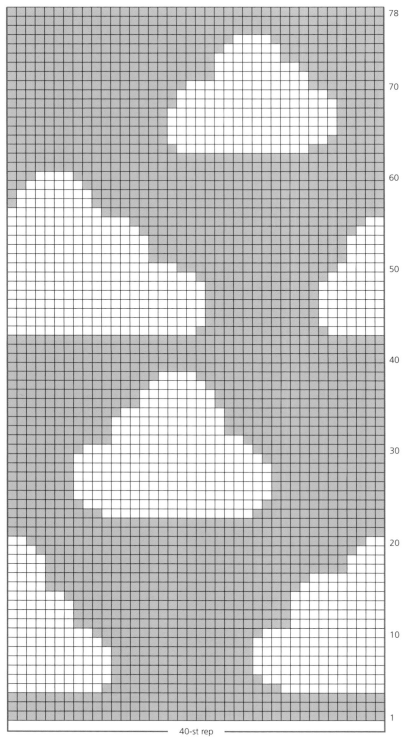

40-st rep

Hello, Houndstooth

Reminiscent of an heirloom quilt, this brightly-colored blanket
features squares knit one quarter at a time, with each new side picked up as you go.

DESIGNED BY AUDREY DRYSDALE

Knitted Measurements
Approx 28 x 28"/71 x 71cm

Materials
▨ 3 3½oz/100g balls (each approx
220yd/200m) of Cascade Yarns *220
Superwash* (superwash wool) in #817
Aran (A) ③
▨ 1 ball each in #850 Lime Sherbet (B),
#836 Pink Ice (C), #1973 Seafoam Heather
(D), and #826 Tangerine (E)
▨ One pair size 7 (4.5mm) needles,
or size to obtain gauges
▨ Size 7 (4.5mm) circular needle,
32"/80cm long

Notes
1) Each square is worked separately in
quarters, then sewn together.
2) Circular needle is used to
accommodate large number of stitches
for borders. Do *not* join.

Blanket
Note See diagram on next page for
visual of block construction.
Make 10 blocks with B as CC, 8 blocks
with C as CC, 9 blocks with D as CC, and
9 blocks with E as CC as foll:

FIRST QUARTER
With CC, cast on 12 sts. Knit 12 rows.
Cut CC and join A.
With A, knit 12 rows. Bind off all sts.

SECOND QUARTER
With RS of first quarter facing and CC,
pick up and k 6 sts along side edge of
CC section of first quarter, and 6 sts
along side edge of A section of first
quarter—12 sts. Knit 11 rows. Cut CC.
With A, knit 12 rows. Bind off all sts.

THIRD QUARTER
With RS of 2nd quarter facing and CC,
pick up and k 6 sts along side edge of
CC section of 2nd quarter, and 6 sts
along side edge of A section of 2nd
quarter—12 sts.
Knit 11 rows. Cut CC.
With A, knit 12 rows. Bind off all sts.

FOURTH QUARTER
With RS of 3rd quarter facing and CC,
pick up and k 6 sts along side edge of
CC section of third quarter, and 6 sts
along side edge of A section of 3rd
quarter—12 sts.
Knit 11 rows. Cut CC.
With A, knit 12 rows. Bind off all sts.
Sew cast-on edge of first quarter to side
edge of fourth quarter.

Gauges
18 sts and 42 rows to 4"/10cm over garter st using size 7 (4.5mm) needles.
1 complete block measures 4½"/11.5cm square
Take time to check gauges.

Hello, Houndstooth

Finishing

Foll assembly diagram, sew blocks into rows. Sew rows together.

BORDERS

With circular needle, A and RS facing, pick up and k 144 sts evenly along one side edge of blanket. Do *not* join.
Knit 4 rows.
Bind off all sts knitwise.
Rep on opposite edge.

With circular needle, A and RS facing, pick up and k 4 sts along side edge of edging, 144 sts evenly along side edge of blanket, and 4 sts along side edge of edging—152 sts.
Knit 4 rows.
Bind off all sts knitwise.
Rep on opposite edge.

Weave in ends.
Block to measurements. ∎

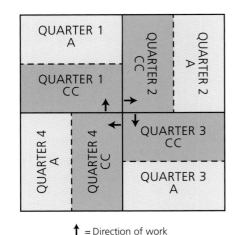

QUARTER 1
A

QUARTER 1
CC

QUARTER 2
CC

QUARTER 2
A

QUARTER 4
A

QUARTER 4
CC

QUARTER 3
CC

QUARTER 3
A

↑ = Direction of work

COLOR KEY
☐ A
☐ B
☐ C
☐ D
☐ E

ASSEMBLY DIAGRAM

Ticking Stripes

This ingenious two-color slip-stitch pattern is knit from corner to corner, using crisp blue and cream for a clean and fresh look.

DESIGNED BY STEVEN HICKS

Knitted Measurements
Approx 25½ x 26"/65 x 66cm

Materials
■ 3 3½oz/100g hanks (each 128yds/117m) of Cascade Yarns *128 Superwash* (superwash merino wool) each in #1944 West Point Blue Heather (A) and #871 White (B) ⑤
■ One size 10 (6mm) circular needle, 32"/80cm long, *or size to obtain gauge*
■ Removable stitch marker

Notes
1) Blanket is worked on the bias, inc and dec along both sides on RS rows.
2) Carry unused color up side of blanket; do *not* cut yarn at end of each stripe.
3) Weave each end into its matching color to maintain reversibility of blanket.

Garter Welt Stitch
(over any number of sts)
Row 1 (WS) With B, knit. Turn.
Row 2 With B, knit, do *not* turn, slide sts to opposite end of needle.
Row 3 With A, knit. Turn.
Row 4 With A, knit, do *not* turn, slide sts to opposite end of needle.
Rep rows 1–4 for garter welt st.

Blanket
With A, cast on 3 sts.
Set-up row Kfb, k1, kfb, do *not* turn, slide sts to opposite end of needle—5 sts. Mark this row as RS of blanket.

BEGIN INCREASES
Row 1 (WS) With B, knit. Turn.
Row 2 With B, kfb, k to last st, kfb, do *not* turn, slide sts to opposite end of needle—2 sts inc'd.
Row 3 With A, knit. Turn.
Row 4 With A, kfb, k to last st, kfb, do *not* turn, slide sts to opposite end of needle—2 sts inc'd.
Rep rows 1–4 thirty-two times more—137 sts.
Work 4 rows even in pat.

BEGIN DECREASES
Row 1 (WS) With B, knit. Turn.
Row 2 With B, ssk, k to last 2 sts, k2tog, do *not* turn, slide sts to opposite end of needle—2 sts dec'd.
Row 3 With A, knit. Turn.
Row 4 With A, ssk, k to last 2 sts, k2tog, do *not* turn, slide sts to opposite end of needle—2 sts dec'd.
Rep rows 1–4 thirty-one times more—9 sts rem.
Next row With B, knit. Turn.
Next row With B, ssk, k to last 2 sts, k2tog, do *not* turn, slide sts to opposite end of needle—7 sts. Cut B.
Next row With A, knit. Turn.
Next row With A, k2tog, [k1, sl first st on RH needle over 2nd st] 3 times, k2tog, sl first st on RH needle over 2nd st—1 st. Cut A and secure last st.

Finishing
Weave in ends.
Block to measurements. ■

Gauge
14 sts and 29 rows to 4"/10cm over garter welt st using size 10 (6mm) needles.
Take time to check gauge

Arrowheads

A sleek triangular design knit in clean modern colors
is just right for a fashion-forward baby.

DESIGNED BY JACOB SEIFERT

Knitted Measurements
Approx 21 x 34"/53.5 x 86.5cm

Materials
■ 4 3½oz/100g hanks (each approx
150yd/138m) of Cascade Yarns *220
Superwash Aran* (superwash merino
wool) in #871 White (A) (4)
■ 1 hank each in #1946 Silver Grey (B)
and #1992 Deep Jungle (C)
■ One size 8 (5mm) circular needle,
40"/100cm long, *or size to obtain gauge*
■ Removable stitch marker

Notes
1) When working wrapped sts, only pick
up wraps if working in a different color;
otherwise simply knit over them.
2) There will always be 4 sts between
wrapped sts.
3) Circular needle is used to
accommodate large number of sts.
Do *not* join.
4) For first solid half-triangle, place a
removable stitch marker to mark right side
of work.

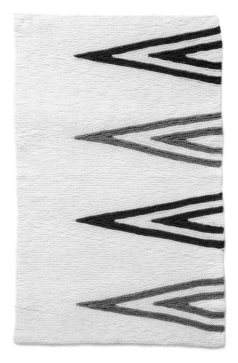

Short Row Wrap & Turn
(w&t)
1) Wyib, sl next st purlwise.
2) Move yarn between needles to front.
3) Sl same st back to LH needle.
Turn work. One st is wrapped.
4) When working wrapped st, insert RH
needle under wrapped st and work it tog
with corresponding st on needle.

Blanket
FIRST SOLID HALF-TRIANGLE
With A, cast on 85 sts.
Row 1 (RS) Knit.
Row 2 (WS) K80, w&t.
Row 3 Knit.
Row 4 K to 5 sts before last wrapped st,
w&t.
Rep last 2 rows 13 times more.
Row 31 Knit.
Row 32 K5, w&t.
Rows 33 and 34 Knit.

STRIPED TRIANGLE
Rows 1 and 2 With A, knit.
Row 3 (RS) K80, w&t.

Gauge
16 sts and 36 rows to 4"/10cm over garter st using size 8 (5mm) needle.
Take time to check gauge.

Row 4 (WS) Knit.
Row 5 K to 5 sts before last wrapped st, w&t.
Row 6 Knit.
With A, rep last 2 rows twice more, [with B, rep last 2 rows 3 times; with A, rep last 2 rows 3 times] twice.
Row 35 With A, k6, w&t.
Row 36 Knit.

Row 37 K to w&t in previous row, k5, w&t.
Row 38 Knit.
With A, rep last 2 rows once more, [with B, rep last 2 rows 3 times; with A, rep last 2 rows 3 times] twice; with A, rep last 2 rows once more.
Rows 67 and 68 With A, knit.

SOLID TRIANGLE
With A only, work as foll:
Row 1 (RS) Knit.
Row 2 (WS) K5, w&t.
Row 3 Knit.
Row 4 K to w&t in previous row, k5, w&t.
Row 5 Knit.
Rep last 2 rows 14 times more.
Rows 34 and 35 Knit.
Row 36 (WS) K80, w&t.
Row 37 Knit.
Row 38 K to 5 sts before last wrapped st, w&t.
Row 39 Knit.
Rep last 2 rows 13 times more.
Row 66 K5, w&t.
Rows 67 and 68 Knit.

Work striped triangle using C instead of B.
Work solid triangle.
Work striped triangle as before with B.
Work solid Triangle.
Work striped triangle using C instead of B.

SECOND SOLID HALF-TRIANGLE
With A only, work as foll:
Row 1 (RS) Knit.
Row 2 (WS) K5, w&t.
Row 3 Knit.
Row 4 K to w&t in previous row, k5, w&t.
Row 5 Knit.
Rep last 2 rows 14 times more.
Row 34 (WS) Knit.
Bind off loosely.

Finishing
Weave in ends.
Block to measurements. ∎

Honeycomb Hexie

Texture and colorwork combine to create a knockout blanket
with a delightful hexagon motif, ready to warm up your little honey.

DESIGNED BY JACQUELINE VAN DILLEN

Knitted Measurements
Approx 26 x 40"/66 x 101.5cm

Materials
- 3 3½oz/100g hanks (each approx 128yd/117m) of Cascade Yarns *128 Superwash* (superwash merino wool) in #817 Ecru (A) **5**
- 4 hanks in #802 Green Apple (B)
- Size 10 (6mm) circular needle, 40"/100cm long, *or size to obtain gauge*

Notes
1) Circular needle is used to accommodate large number of stitches. Do *not* join.
2) Honeycomb Hexie Pattern can be worked from written instructions or chart.

Honeycomb Hexie Pattern
(over a multiple of 8 sts plus 16)
Row 1 (RS) With A, p5 (border sts), k to last 5 sts, p5 (border sts).
Row 2 (WS) With A, p5, k to last 5 sts, p5.
Row 3 With B, p5, k1, *k1, sl 2 wyib, k5; rep from * to last 10 sts, k1, sl 2 wyib, k2, p5.
Short row 4 With B, p7, sl 2 wyif, p1,

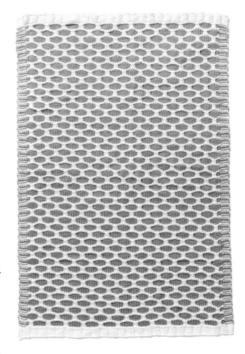

*p5, sl 2 wyif, p1; rep from * to last 6 sts, p1, turn.
Short row 5 With B, sl 1 wyib, *k1, sl 2 wyib, k5; rep from * to last 10 sts, k1, sl 2 wyib, k2, turn.
Short row 6 With B, sl 1 wyif, p1, sl 2 wyif, p1, *p5, sl 2 wyif, p1; rep from * to last 6 sts, p6.
Rows 7 and 8 Rep rows 1 and 2.
Row 9 With B, p5, k1, *k5, sl 2 wyib, k1; rep from * to last 10 sts, k5, p5.
Short row 10 With B, p10, *p1, sl 2 wyif, p5; rep from * to last 6 sts, k1, turn.
Short row 11 With B, sl 1 wyib, *k5, sl 2 wyib, k1; rep from * to last 10 sts, k5, turn.
Short row 12 With B, sl 1 wyif, p4, *p1, sl 2 wyif, p5; rep from * to last 6 sts, p6.
Rows 13 and 14 Rep rows 1 and 2.
Rep rows 3–14 for honeycomb hexie pat.

Blanket
With A, cast on 104 sts.

BOTTOM BORDER
Row 1 (RS) K1, *k2, p2; rep from * to last 3 sts, k3.
Row 2 (WS) P1, *p2, k2; rep from * to last 3 sts, p3.
Rep rows 1 and 2 twice more.

Gauge
14 sts and 26 rows to 4"/10cm over chart pat using size 10 (6mm) needles.
Take time to check gauge.

Honeycomb Hexie

BEGIN PATTERN

Work rows 1–14 of honeycomb hexie pat, work rows 3–14 twenty-one times more, then work rows 3–8 once more. Cut B.

TOP BORDER

With A, work as for bottom border. Bind off in pat.

Finishing

Weave in ends.
Block to measurements. ■

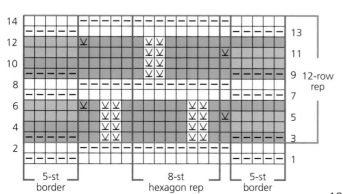

STITCH KEY

- ☐ k on RS, p on WS
- ⊟ p on RS, k on WS
- ⊻ slip 1 wyib on RS, slip 1 wyif on WS
- ▨ short rows, sts not worked

COLOR KEY

- ☐ #817 ecru (A)
- ▨ #802 green apple (B)

18

6 Sly Fox

A clever little fox cavorts across this blanket,
just waiting to take a nap snuggled up with your wee one.

DESIGNED BY AUDREY DRYSDALE

Knitted Measurements
Approx 25 x 25"/63.5 x 63.5cm

Materials
■ 3 3½oz/100g hanks (each approx 150yd/137.5m) of Cascade Yarns *220 Superwash Aran* (superwash merino wool) in #1998 Aqua (A) ④
■ 1 hank each in #822 Pumpkin (B), #900 Charcoal (C), and #817 Aran (D)
■ One size 8 (5mm) circular needle, 32"/80cm long, *or size to obtain gauge*
■ Stitch markers

Notes
1) Chart is worked using intarsia method. Use a separate ball of color for each color section. When changing colors, twist yarns on WS to prevent holes in work.
2) Charts are worked in Stockinette stitch (k on RS, p on WS).
3) Circular needle is used to accommodate large number of stitches. Do *not* join.

Blanket
With A, cast on 115 sts.
Row 1 (RS) K1, *p1, k1; rep from * to end.
Row 2 (WS) P1, *k1, p1; rep from * to end.

Row 3 Rep row 2.
Row 4 Rep row 1.
Rep rows 1–4 for double moss st, then rep rows 1 and 2 once more.
Row 11 Work 9 sts in double moss st as established, pm, k to last 9 sts, pm, work 9 sts in double moss st as established.
Row 12 Work 9 sts in double moss st, sm, p to last 9 sts, sm, work 9 sts in double moss st.
Rep last 2 rows 5 times more.

BEGIN CHART
Row 1 (RS) Work 9 sts in double moss st, sm, work chart 1 (first half) over 50 sts, work chart 1 (second half) over 47 sts, sm, work 9 sts in double moss st.
Row 2 Work 9 sts in double moss st, sm, work chart 2 (second half) over 47 sts, work chart 1 (first half) over 50 sts, sm, work 9 sts in double moss st.
Working 9 sts each side in double moss st and both halves of chart 1 as established, work through row 50, then work both halves of chart 2 through row 101.
Cont with A only, work as foll:
Next row (WS) Work 9 sts in double moss st, sm, p to last 9 sts, sm, work 9 sts in double moss st.
Next row (RS) Work 9 sts in double moss st, sm, k to last 9 sts, sm, work 9 sts in double moss st.
Rep last 2 rows until piece measures 23"/58.5cm from beg, end with a WS row. Work 10 rows in double moss st over all sts. Bind off in pat.

Finishing
Weave in ends.
Block to measurements. ■

Gauge
18 sts and 24 rows to 4"/10cm over St st using size 8 (5mm) needle.
Take time to check gauge.

Sly Fox

CHART 1 (SECOND HALF)

COLOR KEY

A   B

C   D

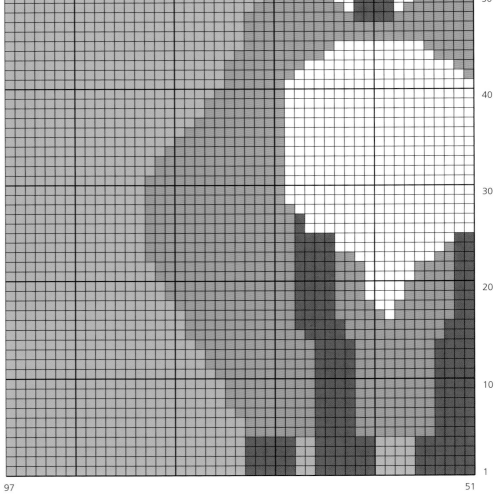

97   51

22

CHART 1 (FIRST HALF)

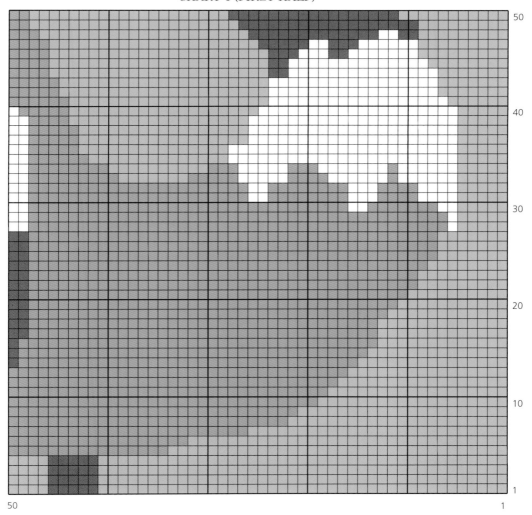

Sly Fox

CHART 2 (SECOND HALF)

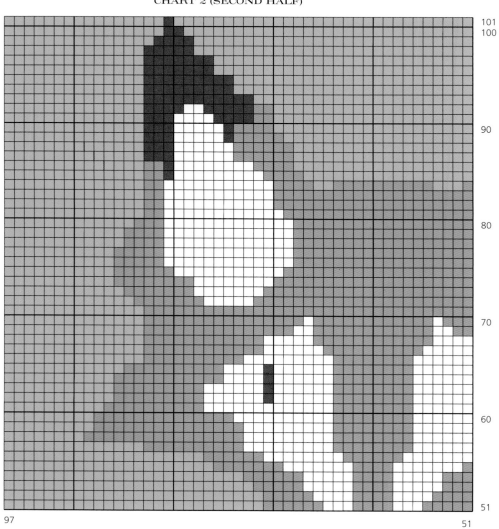

COLOR KEY

A   B

C   D

CHART 2 (FIRST HALF)

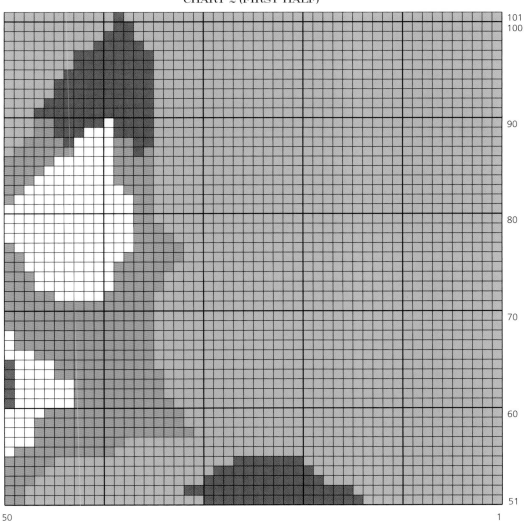

Bon-Bon

Stripes of chocolate and strawberry
make this blanket deliciously sweet–and cuddly warm, too.

DESIGNED BY KATHARINE MEHLS

Knitted Measurements
Approx 16 x 28"/40.5 x 71cm

Materials
■ 2 3½oz/100g balls (each approx 220yd/200m) of Cascade Yarns *220 Superwash* (superwash wool) each in #835 Pink Rose (A) and #818 Mocha (B) **3**
■ Two size 7 (4.5mm) circular needles, 36"/90cm long, *or size to obtain gauge*
■ Stitch markers

Broken Garter Stripe
(over a multiple of 4 sts plus 2)
Rows 1, 3, 5, and 7 (RS) With B, knit.
Rows 2, 4, 6, and 8 With B, p1, *p1, k3; rep from * to last st, p1.
Rows 9, 11, 13, and 15 With A, knit.
Rows 10, 12, 14, and 16 With A, p1, k2, *p1, k3; rep from * to last 3 sts, p1, k1, p1.
Rep rows 1–16 for broken garter stripe.

Notes
1) Circular needles are used to accommodate large number of stitches on I-cord edging. Do *not* join.
2) Carry yarn not in use along side of blanket when changing colors.

Blanket
With B, cast on 86 sts.
Work rows 1–16 of broken garter stripe 16 times, then work rows 1–8 once more. Turn to work RS row, cut B.
With RS facing and A, knit across row, pm, pick up and k 1 st in every garter ridge along left edge, pm, pick up and k 1 st in every st of cast-on edge, pm, pick up and k 1 st in every garter row along right edge.

I-CORD EDGING
Using cable cast-on and A, cast on 4 sts to LH needle.
*Next row (RS) K3, k2tog tbl (the last cast-on st tog with the next st on RH needle), sl these 4 sts back to LH needle, pull yarn snug across back of work.
Rep last row and work across sts to next marker. Turn work.
Corner row (WS) P4. Turn work.
Rep from * 3 times more, removing markers. Turn work and bind off rem sts purlwise. Sew ends of I-cord tog.

Finishing
Weave in ends.
Block to measurements. ■

Gauge
23 sts and 38 rows to 4"/10cm over broken garter stripe using size 7 (4.5mm) needle.
Take time to check gauge.

Tumbling Blocks

It's said that quilts with a tumbling blocks pattern were used as symbols on the Underground Railroad. This knitted version will make a treasured gift.

DESIGNED BY CLEO MALONE

Knitted Measurements
Approx 25½ x 22"/65 x 56cm

Materials
■ 3 3½oz/100g balls (each approx 220yd/200m) of Cascade Yarns *220 Superwash* (superwash wool) in #821 Daffodil ④
■ Size 7 (4.5mm) circular needle, 32"/80cm long, *or size to obtain gauge*
■ Stitch markers

Note
Circular needle is used to accommodate large number of stitches. Do *not* join.

Seed Stitch
(over an even number of sts)
Row 1 (RS) *K1, p1; rep from * to end.
Row 2 *P1, k1; rep from * to end.
Rep rows 1 and 2 for seed st.

Blanket
Cast on 140 sts. Work 4 rows in seed st.

BEGIN CHART
Row 1 (RS) Work 7 sts in seed st as established, pm, work 14-st chart rep 9 times, pm, work 7 sts in seed st as established.

Row 2 Work in seed st to marker, sm, work chart pat as established to marker, sm, work in seed st to end.

Cont pats in this manner until rows 1–26 of chart have been worked 7 times, then work chart rows 1–14 once more.
Work 4 rows in seed st. Bind off in pat.

Finishing
Weave in ends.
Block to measurements. ■

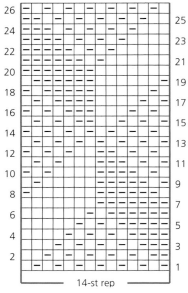

14-st rep

STITCH KEY
☐ k on RS, p on WS
— p on RS, k on WS

Gauge
22 sts and 34 rows to 4"/10cm over chart using size 7 (4.5mm) needle.
Take time to check gauge.

9 Gooseberries

Elegant cabled panels set off a center worked in an Estonian cluster stitch, creating an exquisite blanket sure to become a family heirloom.

DESIGNED BY BROOKE NICO

Knitted Measurements
Approx 23 x 35"/58.5 x 90cm

Materials
■ 4 3½oz/100g balls (each approx 220yd/200m) of Cascade Yarns *220 Superwash* (superwash wool) in #250 Laurel Green 〈4〉
■ One pair size 8 (5mm) needles, *or size to obtain gauge*
■ Cable needle (cn)
■ Stitch markers

Stitch Glossary
2-st RC Sl 1 st to cn and hold to *back*, k1, k1 from cn.
2-st LC Sl 1 st to cn and hold to *front*, k1, k1 from cn.
4-st RPC Sl 1 st to cn and hold to *back*, k3, p1 from cn.
4-st LPC Sl 3 sts to cn and hold to *front*, p1, k3 from cn.
4-st RC Sl 2 sts to cn and hold to *back*, k2, k2 from cn.
4-st LC Sl 2 sts to cn and hold to *front*, k2, k2 from cn.
WC (wrapped cluster) Work over 3 sts as foll: pass 3rd st on LH needle over first 2 sts, k1, yo, k1.

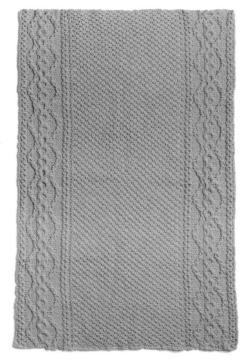

WC LPC (wrapped cluster LPC) Sl 3 sts to cn and hold to *front*, p1, sl 3 sts from cn to LH needle, WC.
WC RPC (wrapped cluster RPC) Sl 1 st to cn and hold to *back*, WC, p1 from cn.

Cable Panel
(over 34 sts)
Row 1 (RS) P1, 2-st RC, 2-st LC, p5, WC, 4-st LC, 4-st RC, WC, p5, 2-st RC, 2-st LC, p1.
Row 2 (WS) K1, p4, k5, p14, k5, p4, k1.
Row 3 P1, 2-st LC, 2-st RC, p4, 4-st RPC, k8, 4-st LPC, p4, 2-st LC, 2-st RC, p1.
Row 4 K1, p4, k4, p3, k1, p8, k1, p3, k4, p4, k1.
Row 5 P1, 2-st RC, 2-st LC, p3, WC RPC, p1, 4-st RC, 4-st LC, p1, WC LPC, p3, 2-st RC, 2-st LC, p1.
Row 6 K1, p4, k3, p3, k2, p8, k2, p3, k3, p4, k1.
Row 7 P1, 2-st LC, 2-st RC, p2, 4-st RPC, p2, k8, p2, 4-st LPC, p2, 2-st LC, 2-st RC, p1.
Row 8 K1, p4, k2, p3, k3, p8, k3, p3, k2, p4, k1.
Row 9 P1, 2-st RC, 2-st LC, p1, WC RPC, p3, 4-st LC, 4-st RC, p3, WC LPC, p1, 2-st RC, 2-st LC, p1.

Gauge
23 sts and 28 rows to 4"/10cm over allover berry st using size 8 (5mm) needles.
Take time to check gauge.

Gooseberries

Row 10 K1, p4, k1, p3, k4, p8, k4, p3, k1, p4, k1.
Row 11 P1, 2-st LC, 2-st RC, p1, k3, p4, k8, p4, k3, p1, 2-st LC, 2-st RC, p1.
Row 12 Rep row 10.
Row 13 P1, 2-st RC, 2-st LC, p1, WC, p4, 4-st RC, 4-st LC, p4, WC, p1, 2-st RC, 2-st LC, p1.
Row 14 Rep row 10.
Row 15 P1, 2-st LC, 2-st RC, p1, 4-st LPC, p3, k8, p3, 4-st RPC, p1, 2-st LC, 2-st RC, p1.
Row 16 Rep row 8.
Row 17 P1, 2-st RC, 2-st LC, p2, WC LPC, p2, 4-st LC, 4-st RC, p2, WC RPC, p2, 2-st RC, 2-st LC, p1.
Row 18 Rep row 6.
Row 19 P1, 2-st LC, 2-st RC, p3, 4-st LPC, p1, k8, p1, 4-st RPC, p3, 2-st LC, 2-st RC, p1.
Row 20 Rep row 4.
Row 21 P1, 2-st RC, 2-st LC, p4, WC LPC,

4-st RC, 4-st LC, WC RPC, p4, 2-st RC, 2-st LC, p1.
Row 22 Rep row 2.
Row 23 P1, 2-st LC, 2-st RC, p5, k14, p5, 2-st LC, 2-st RC, p1.
Row 24 Rep row 2.
Rep rows 1–24 for cable panel.

Allover Berry Stitch
(over a multiple of 4 sts plus 3)
Row 1 (RS) *WC, k1; rep from *, end WC.
Row 2 Purl.
Row 3 K2, *WC, k1; rep from *, end k1.
Row 4 Purl.
Rep rows 1–4 for allover berry st.

Note
Cable panel can be worked from written instructions or chart.

Blanket
Cast on 133 sts.

BEGIN PATTERNS
Set-up row (WS) P1, *k1, p4, k5, p14, p5, p4, k1*, pm, p63, pm, rep from * to *, p1.
Next row (RS) K1, work row 1 of cable panel over 34 sts, sm, work row 1 of allover berry pat over center 63 sts, sm, work row 1 of cable panel over 34 sts, k1.
Next row P1, work row 2 of cable panel, sm, work row 2 of allover berry pat to next marker, sm, work row 2 of cable panel, p1. Work as established, keeping first and last sts in rev St st (p on RS, K on WS), cont through row 24 of cable panel, then work rows 1–24 eight times more, then work rows 1–22 once.
Bind off loosely in pat.

Finishing
Weave in ends.
Block to measurements. ■

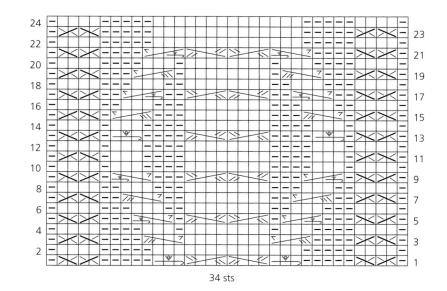

34 sts

STITCH KEY

☐		k on RS, p on WS
⊟		p on RS, k on WS
		2-st RC
		2-st LC
		4-st RC
		4-st LC
		4-st RPC
		4-st LPC
		WC
		WC RPC
		WC LPC

10

All My Love

Made from hugs and kisses, this fun blanket will wrap up baby in love.

DESIGNED BY THERESA SCHABES

Knitted Measurements
Approx 33½ x 33½"/85 x 85cm

Materials
■ 4 3½oz/100g balls (each approx 220yd/200m) of Cascade Yarns *220 Superwash* (superwash wool) in #817 Aran (A) (3)
■ 2 balls each in #849 Dark Aqua (B) and #908 Magenta (C)
■ One pair size 6 (4mm) needles, *or size to obtain gauge*
■ One size 6 (4mm) circular needle, 40"/100cm long
■ Removable stitch markers

Notes
1) Circular needle is used to accommodate large number of border stitches. Do *not* join.
2) When working blocks, leave 10"/25.5cm tails for seaming.

Blanket
A AND B SQUARES (MAKE 20)
With B, cast on 3 sts.

Begin increases
Row 1 (WS) K3.

Row 2 (RS) K1, [k into front, back, and front of next st] once, k1—5 sts. Mark this row as RS.
Row 3 K5.
Row 4 K1, kfb, k to last 2 sts, kfb, k1—2 sts inc'd.
Row 5 Knit.
Rep rows 4 and 5 until there are 19 sts, end with a row 5. Cut A, join B.
Rep rows 4 and 5 until there are 37 sts, end with a row 5.

Begin decreases
Row 1 (RS) K1, ssk, k to last 3 sts, k2tog, k1—2 sts dec'd.
Row 2 (WS) Knit.
Rep rows 1 and 2 until there are 21 sts, end with a row 2. Cut B, join A.
Rep rows 1 and 2 until there are 5 sts, end with a row 2.
Next row (RS) K1, k3tog, k1—3 sts.
Next row Knit.
Next row K3tog—1 st.
Bind off rem st.

A AND C SQUARES (MAKE 16)
With A cast on 3 sts. Work as for A and B squares, substituting C for B.

Finishing
ASSEMBLY
Foll diagram (see next page) to arrange 4 A and B squares to form an X. Seam with mattress st. Rep to make 4 more X squares.
Foll diagram and arrange 4 A and C squares to form an O. Seam with mattress st. Rep to make 3 more O squares.
Foll diagram to arrange all X and 0 squares into blanket. Seam with mattress st.

Gauge
21 sts and 46 rows to 4"/10cm over garter st using size 6 (4mm) needles.
Take time to check gauge.

10 All My Love

BORDER

With A, beg at any corner, pick up and k 1 st in corner st, *pick up and k 108 sts evenly across blanket edge to next corner, pick up and k 1 st in corner st, pm, pick up and k another st in same corner st; rep from * twice more, pick up and k 108 sts evenly across blanket edge to next corner, pick up and k 1 st in corner st, pm for beg of rnd—440 sts. Join to work in the rnd.

Rnd 1 Purl.

Rnd 2 *Kfb in corner st, k to 1 st before marker, kfb in corner st, sm; rep from * to end of rnd—8 sts inc'd.

Rep rnds 1 and 2 until edging measures 2½"/5.5 cm, end with a rnd 2.

Turn work and bind off on WS.

Weave in ends.
Block to measurements. ■

Assembly Diagram

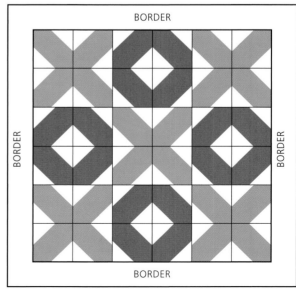

COLOR KEY
☐ A ▨ B ■ C

11

Baby Spider Web

Softly dappled yarn and a circular shape give baby a cozy "web" to cuddle up in.

DESIGNED BY CHERI ESPER

Knitted Measurements
Diameter Approx 30"/76cm

Materials
▓ 4 3½oz/100g hanks (each approx 150yd/137.5m) of Cascade Yarns *220 Superwash Aran Splatter* (superwash merino wool) in #01 Lilacs (4)
▓ One size 9 (5.5mm) circular needle, 16, 24 and 32"/40, 60 and 80cm long, *or size to obtain gauge*
▓ One set of 5 size 9 (5.5mm) double-pointed needles (dpn)
▓ Stitch marker

Note
Begin with longest circular needle and change to shorter needles, and eventually to dpn, when sts no longer fit comfortably on each needle.

Blanket
With longest circular needle, cast on 400 sts. Join, taking care not to twist sts, and pm for beg of rnd.
Rnds 1–4 [K20, p20] 10 times.

Dec rnd 5 [Ssk, k16, k2tog, p2tog, p16, ssp] 10 times—360 sts.
Rnds 6–14 [K18, p18] 10 times.
Dec rnd 15 [Ssk, k14, k2tog, p2tog, p14, ssp] 10 times—320 sts.
Rnds 16–24 [K16, p16] 10 times.
Dec rnd 25 [Ssk, k12, k2tog, p2tog, p12, ssp] 10 times—280 sts.
Rnds 26–34 [K14, p14] 10 times.

Dec rnd 35 [Ssk, k10, k2tog, p2tog, p10, ssp] 10 times—240 sts.
Rnds 36–44 [K12, p12] 10 times.
Dec rnd 45 [Ssk, k8, k2tog, p2tog, p8, ssp] 10 times—200 sts.
Rnds 46–54 [K10, p10] 10 times.
Dec rnd 55 [Ssk, k6, k2tog, p2tog, p6, ssp] 10 times—160 sts.
Rnds 56–64 [K8, p8] 10 times.
Dec rnd 65 [Ssk, k4, k2tog, p2tog, p4, ssp] 10 times—120 sts.
Rnds 66–74 [K6, p6] 10 times.
Dec rnd 75 [Ssk, k2, k2tog, p2tog, p2, ssp] 10 times—80 sts.
Rnds 76–84 [K4, p4] 10 times.
Dec rnd 85 [Ssk, k2tog, p2tog, ssp] 10 times—40 sts.
Rnds 86–88 [K2, p2] 10 times.
Dec rnd 89 [Ssk, ssp] 10 times—20 sts.
Rnds 90–91 [K1, p1] 10 times.
Dec rnd 92 [K2tog, p2tog] 5 times—10 sts.
Cut yarn and pull through rem sts twice, draw up and secure.

Finishing
Weave in ends.
Block to measurements. ■

Gauge
17 sts and 24½ rows to 4"/10cm over St st using size 9 (5.5mm) needles.
Take time to check gauge.

Buttercups

Scalloped edges and looping cables create
a wildflower meadow for your little one.

DESIGNED BY KATHARINE HUNT

Knitted Measurements
Approx 21 x 35"/53.5 x 90cm

Materials
■ 5 3½oz/100g hanks (each approx
150yd/137.5m) of Cascade Yarns *220
Superwash Aran* (superwash merino wool)
in #820 Lemon ■
■ One size 9 (5.5mm) circular needle,
36"/91.5cm long, *or size to obtain gauge*
■ Cable needle (cn)

Notes
1) Cable and scallop pat can be worked
from written instructions or chart.
2) Circular needle is used to
accommodate large number of stitches.
Do *not* join.

Stitch Glossary
6-st RC Sl 3 sts to cn and hold to *back*,
k3, k3 from cn.

Cable and Scallop Pattern
(over a multiple of 18 sts plus 18)
Row 1 (RS) [K2tog] 3 times, *[yo, k1] 6
times, [k2tog] 6 times; rep from * to last

12 sts, [yo, k1] 6 times, [k2tog] 3 times.
Row 2 P3, k12, *p6, k12; rep from * to
last 3 sts, p3.
Row 3 K3, *k12, 6-st RC; rep from * to
last 15 sts, k15.
Row 4 Purl.
Rows 5 and 6 Rep rows 1 and 2.
Row 7 Knit.
Row 8 Purl.
Rep rows 1–8 for cable and scallop pat.

Blanket
BOTTOM BORDER
Cast on 114 sts.
Row 1 (RS) Knit.
Dec row 2 K2tog, k to last 2 sts, k2tog
—2 sts dec'd.
Rep last 2 rows twice more—108 sts.
Next row (RS) Knit.
Next row Purl.
Border measures approx 1"/2.5cm from beg.

BEGIN PATTERN
Work cable and scallop pat, rep rows 1–8
until piece measures approx 34"/86.5cm
from beg, end with pat row 7.

Gauge
23 sts and 24 rows to 4"/10cm over cable and scallop pat using size 9 (5.5mm) needles, after blocking.
Take time to check gauge

12 Buttercups

TOP BORDER
Next dec row (WS) Kfb, [k16, ssk] 5 times, k16, kfb—105 sts.
Next row (RS) Knit.
Next inc row Kfb, k to last st, kfb —2 sts inc'd.
Rep last 2 rows once more—109 sts.
Next row (RS) Knit.
Bind off.

SIDE BORDERS
With RS facing, work along one side edge of cable and scallop pat only, pick up and k approx 19 sts every 4"/10cm. Do *not* pick up sts along top and bottom borders.
Next inc row (WS) Kfb, k to last st, kfb —2 sts inc'd.
Next row (RS) Knit.
Rep last 2 rows twice more.
Bind off on WS.
Rep along other side edge.

Finishing
Seam corner edges of borders tog.
Weave in ends.
Block to measurements, pinning scalloped edges into shape. ∎

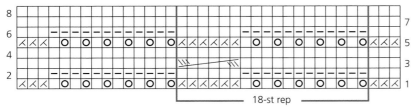

STITCH KEY

☐ k on RS, p on WS

⊟ p on RS, k on WS

Ⓞ yo

◩ k2tog

6-st RC

Pinwheels

Modular knitting is just the ticket for creating this clever pinwheel effect:
each square is made of four triangles, showing off splatter-dyed yarns to perfection.

DESIGNED BY DEBBIE O'NEILL

Knitted Measurements
Approx 28 x 41½"/70 x 105.5cm

Materials
▪ 4 3½oz/100g hanks (each approx 150yd/137.5m) of Cascade Yarns *220 Superwash Aran Splatter* (superwash merino wool) each in #06 Tempest (A) and #05 Stormy Seas (B) 🔲4🔲
▪ One pair size 8 (5mm) needles, *or size to obtain gauge*
▪ One size 8 (5mm) circular needle, 36"/90cm long

Notes
1) Each pinwheel consists of 2 A triangles and 2 B triangles, which are picked up and knitted in sequence (see pinwheel diagram on next page). Six completed pinwheels are seamed tog to form blanket.
2) Circular needle is used to accommodate large number of stitches on borders. Do *not* join.

Blanket
PINWHEEL (MAKE 6)
Triangle 1
With A and straight needles, cast on 39 sts.
Set-up row (WS) Knit.

Dec row 1 (RS) K2tog, k to end—1 st dec'd.
Row 2 Knit.
Rep rows 1 and 2 until 2 sts rem, end with a row 2.
Next row K2tog—1 st. Fasten off rem st.

Triangle 2
With A, straight needles, RS facing, and working along left side edge of triangle 1 (end of RS rows) from last row to cast-on row, pick up and k 39 sts.
Set-up row (WS) Knit.
Row 1 (RS) K2tog, k to end—1 st dec'd
Row 2 Knit.
Complete as for triangle 1. Cut A.

Triangle 3
With B, straight needles and RS facing, pick up and k 39 sts along left side edge of triangle 2. Complete as for triangle 1. Cut B.

Triangle 4
With B, straight needles and RS facing, pick up and k 39 sts along left side edge of triangle 3. Complete as for triangle 1. Cut B, leaving tail for seaming.
Seam cast-on edge of triangle 1 to side edge of triangle 4 to complete square.

Finishing
ASSEMBLY
Foll assembly diagram (see next page) to assemble squares in pinwheel design and seam tog.

Gauge
16 sts and 32 rows to 4"/10cm over garter st using 8 (5mm) needles.
Take time to check gauge.

Pinwheels

BORDERS

With A, circular needle, and RS facing, pick up and k 120 sts evenly along left side edge of blanket. Knit 6 rows. Bind off loosely on WS.

In same manner, pick up and k 84 sts evenly along lower edge, including side border. Knit 6 rows. Bind off loosely on WS. In same manner, pick up and k 124 sts evenly along right side edge, including the lower edge border. Knit 6 rows. Bind off loosely on WS. In same manner, pick up and k 88 sts evenly along top edge, including both borders. Knit 6 rows. Bind off loosely on WS.

Weave in ends. Block to measurements. ■

ASSEMBLY DIAGRAM

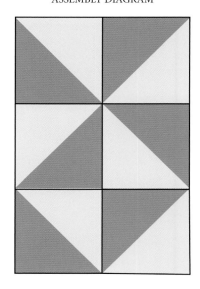

PINWHEEL DIAGRAM

COLOR KEY
- ■ A
- ☐ B

TRIANGLE 2
TRIANGLE 1
TRIANGLE 3
TRIANGLE 4

↑ = Direction of work

◀ - - = Pick-up edge and direction of pick-up

▬ = Cast on edge

Zigzag Zoom

A zigzag pattern knit in the colors of sunshine will brighten the nursery.
Start at one corner and build each chevron diagonally, changing colors as you go.

DESIGNED BY THERESA SCHABES

Knitted Measurements
Approx 25 x 34"/63.5 x 86.5cm

Materials
■ 2 3½oz/100g balls (each approx 220yd/200m) of Cascade Yarns *220 Superwash* (superwash wool) each in #910A Winter White (A), #821 Daffodil (B), #827 Coral (C), and #907 Tangerine Heather (D) 🧶
■ One size 6 (4mm) circular needle, 32"/80cm long, *or size to obtain gauge*
■ One size 6 (4mm) double-pointed needle (dpn)
■ 8 stitch markers, 4 each in 2 different colors

Notes
1) In garter stitch, one ridge equals 2 rows.
2) Yarn tails at edges can be woven into center of I-cord edging while finishing.
3) Use markers in one color to indicate inside, or decrease, corners, and markers in a different color to indicate outside, or increase, corners.
4) When picking up sts in garter ridges along side edges, pick up 1 st for each garter ridge.

Blanket
CHEVRON 1
With A, cast on 16 sts. Knit 32 rows, end with a WS row.
Cut yarn.

CHEVRON 2
Row 1 (RS) With C, k15, [kfb, pm, kfb] in next st, turn and pick up 15 sts along side edge of chevron 1—34 sts.
Row 2 (WS) Knit.
Row 3 K to 1 st before marker, kfb, sm, kfb, k to end—2 sts inc'd.
Rep rows 2 and 3 fourteen times more, then rep row 2 once more—64 sts.
Cut yarn.

CHEVRON 3
Row 1 (RS) With B, cast on 47 sts, pm, working across C sts, k2tog, k to 1 st before marker, kfb, sm, kfb, k to last 2 sts, ssk, pm, cast on 47 sts—158 sts.
Row 2 (WS) Knit.
Row 3 K to 2 sts before marker, ssk, sm, k2tog, k to 1 st before marker, kfb, sm, kfb, k to 2 sts before marker, ssk, sm, k2tog, k to end—2 sts dec'd.
Rep rows 2 and 3 fourteen times more, then rep row 2 once more—128 sts. Cut yarn.

CHEVRON 4
Row 1 (RS) With D, pick up and k 15 sts along right edge of chevron 3, working across C sts, [kfb, pm, kfb] in next st, k

Gauge
20 sts and 40 rows to 4"/10cm over garter st using size 6 (4mm) needles.
Take time to check gauge.

Zigzag Zoom

to 2 sts before marker, ssk, sm, k2tog, k to 1 st before marker, kfb, sm, kfb, k to 2 sts before marker, ssk, sm, k2tog, k to last st, [kfb, pm, kfb] in next st, turn and pick up and k 15 sts along left edge of chevron 3—162 sts.
Row 2 (WS) Knit.
Row 3 *K to 1 st before marker, kfb, sm, kfb, k to 2 sts before marker, ssk, sm, k2tog; rep from * once more, k to 1 st before marker, kfb, sm, kfb, k to end—2 sts inc'd. Rep rows 2 and 3 fourteen times more, then rep row 2 once more—192 sts.
Cut yarn.

CHEVRON 5
Row 1 (RS) With A, cast on 47 sts, pm, working across D sts, k2tog, *k to 1 st before marker, kfb, sm, kfb, k to 2 sts before marker, ssk, sm, k2tog; rep from * once more, k to 1 st before marker, kfb, sm, kfb, k to last 2 sts, ssk, pm, cast on 31 sts—270 sts.
Row 2 (WS) Knit.
Row 3 *K to 2 sts before marker, ssk, sm, k2tog, k to 1 st before marker, kfb, sm, kfb; rep from * twice more, k to 2 sts before marker, ssk, sm, k2tog, k to end—2 sts dec'd. Rep rows 2 and 3 fourteen times more, then rep row 2 once more—240 sts.
Cut yarn.

CHEVRON 6
Row 1 (RS) With C, pick up and k 15 sts along right edge of chevron 5, working across A sts, [kfb, pm, kfb] in next st, *k to 2 sts before marker, ssk, sm, k2tog, k to 1 st before marker, kfb, sm, kfb; rep from * twice more, k to 2 sts before marker, ssk, sm, k2tog, k to end—256 sts.
Row 2 (WS) Knit.
Row 3 *K to 1 st before marker, kfb, sm, kfb, k to 2 sts before marker, ssk, sm, k2tog;

rep from * three more times, k to end. Rep rows 2 and 3 thirteen times more, then rep row 2 once more.
Next row (RS) Work row 3 as before to last 3 sts, removing last marker, SK2P—2 sts dec'd.
Next row (WS) Bind off to first marker, k to end—224 sts.
Cut yarn.

CHEVRON 7
Row 1 (RS) With B, *k to 1 st before marker, kfb, sm, kfb, k to 2 sts before marker, ssk, sm, k2tog; rep from * twice more, k to end.
Row 2 (WS) Knit.
Rep rows 1 and 2 fourteen times more, then work row 1 once more.
Next row (WS) K to last marker, remove marker and bind off rem sts—176 sts.
Cut yarn.

CHEVRON 8
Row 1 (RS) With D, *k to 2 sts before marker, ssk, sm, k2tog, k to 1 st before marker, kfb, sm, kfb; rep from * once more, k to 2 sts before marker, ssk, sm, k2tog, k to end—2 sts dec'd.
Row 2 (WS) Knit.
Rep rows 2 and 3 fourteen times more.

Next row (RS) Work row 1 as before to last 3 sts, removing last marker, SK2P.
Next row (WS) Bind off to first marker, k to end—112 sts.
Cut yarn.

CHEVRON 9
Row 1 (RS) With A, *k to 2 sts before marker, ssk, sm, k2tog, k to 1 st before marker, kfb, sm, kfb, k to 2 sts before marker, ssk, sm, k2tog, k to end—2 sts dec'd.
Row 2 (WS) Knit.
Rep rows 1 and 2 fourteen times more, then work row 1 once more—80 sts.
Next row (WS) K to 2nd marker, remove marker and bind off rem sts—48 sts.
Cut yarn.

CHEVRON 10
Row 1 (RS) With C, *k to 2 sts before marker, ssk, sm, k2tog, k to end—2 sts dec'd.
Row 2 (WS) Knit.
Rep rows 1 and 2 fourteen times more.
Next row (RS) Work to last 3 sts, removing last marker, SK2P—16 sts.
Bind off rem sts.

Finishing
I-CORD EDGING
With RS facing and D, pick up and k 1 st for each ridge or each st along each blanket edge.
Cast on 4 sts to left side of circular needle. With dpn, *k3, ssk, sl 4 sts back to LH needle, pull yarn tightly behind work; rep from * to corner, then work three I-cord rows into corner st.
Cont to work edging in this manner along rem 3 edges.
Bind off rem sts and seam ends of I-cord tog.

Weave in ends.
Block to measurements. ■

15

Checkered Blocks

A riot of cheerful colors gives this blanket the feel of a patchwork quilt
while the checkerboard pattern provides textural charm.

DESIGNED BY JACQUELINE VAN DILLEN

Knitted Measurements
Approx 26¼ x 41¼"/66.5 x 105cm

Materials
■ 1 3½oz/100g ball (each approx 220yd/200m) of Cascade Yarns *220 Superwash* (superwash wool) each in #837 Berry Pink (A), #1942 Mint (B), #835 Pink Rose (C), #824 Yellow (D), #1960 Pacific (E), #877 Golden (F), #1952 Blaze (G), #847 Caribbean (H), #906 Chartreuse (I), #1921 Persimmon (J), and #886 Citron (K) ④
■ One pair size 6 (4mm) needles, *or size to obtain gauges*
■ Two size 6 (4mm) double-pointed needles (dpn) for edging

Note
Five strips of seven blocks each are made separately, then seamed together.

Pattern Stitch
(over a multiple of 3 sts plus 3)
Rows 1 and 3 (RS) K1, *p1, k2; rep from * to last 2 sts, p1, k1.
Row 2 (WS) K2, *p2, k1; rep from * to last st, k1.
Row 4 Knit.
Rep rows 1–4 for pat st.

Blanket
FIRST STRIP
With A, cast on 36 sts. Work rows 1–4 of pat st 12 times (one block complete). Work 6 blocks more in color sequence as foll: C, I, G, E, H and F. Bind off.

SECOND STRIP
Work as for first strip, working blocks in E, K, F, H, D, A, and G.

THIRD STRIP
Work as for first strip, working blocks in F, H, B, J, K, C, and E.

FOURTH STRIP
Work as for first strip, working blocks in J, D, E, I, B, G, and A.

FIFTH STRIP
Work as for first strip, working blocks in B, A, G, C, F, I, and H.

Finishing
Using assembly diagram as guide (see next page), beg with first strip at left edge, seam strips tog.

Gauges
24 sts and 33 rows to 4"/10cm over pat st using size 6 (4mm) needles.
Each block measures 6 x 6"/15 x 15cm.
Take time to check gauges.

Checkered Blocks

I-CORD EDGING

With dpn and K, cast on 4 sts. *Slide sts to opposite end of dpn, pulling yarn tightly behind work, k3, sl 1, pick up 1 st from blanket edge and ssk tog with slipped st; rep from *, working evenly around all 4 edges of blanket. Sew last row to first row.

Weave in ends.
Block to measurements. ■

ASSEMBLY DIAGRAM

H	A	E	G	F
I	G	C	A	H
F	B	K	D	E
C	I	J	H	G
G	E	B	F	I
A	D	H	K	C
B	J	F	E	A

| 5 | 4 | 3 | 2 | 1 |

COLOR KEY

A	E	I
B	F	J
C	G	K
D	H	

16

Sleepy Sheep

Gray and white sheep, knitted intarsia-style, frolic across this adorable blanket
—the perfect project for a knitter and her favorite little lamb.

DESIGNED BY JACOB SEIFERT

■◀■■▷

Knitted Measurements
Approx 23 x 21½"/58.5 x 54.5cm

Materials
■ 2 3½oz/100g hanks (each approx 150yd/137.5m) of Cascade Yarns *220 Superwash Aran* (superwash merino wool) in #1946 Silver Grey (A) (4)
■ 1 hank each in #817 Aran (B) and #815 Black (C)
■ One pair size 8 (5mm) needles, *or size to obtain gauge*
■ Stitch markers

Notes
1) Use a separate ball for each section of color, twisting yarns on the wrong side when changing colors.
2) Sheep charts are worked over an odd number of rows.
Chart 1 always begins on a WS row.
Chart 2 always begins on a RS row.
3) Charts are worked in St st (k on RS, p on WS).

Double Seed Stitch
(over a multiple of 2 sts plus 1)
Row 1 (RS) K1, *p1, k1; rep from * to end.

Row 2 (WS) P1, *k1, p1; rep from * to end.
Row 3 P1, *k1, p1; rep from * to end.
Row 4 K1, *p1, k1; rep from * to end.
Rep rows 1–4 for double seed st.

Blanket
BOTTOM BORDER
With A, cast on 87 sts.
Row 1 (RS) Sl 1 st (selvage st), work in double seed st to last st, k1 (selvage st). Rep row 1 for approx 2"/5cm, ending with a RS row. Cut A.

FIRST STRIPE AND SHEEP
Join B.
Row 1 (WS) With B, sl 1 st (selvage st), pm, work row 1 of chart 1, pm, p to last st, k1 (selvage st).
Row 2 (RS) Sl 1 st (selvage st), k to marker, sm, work row 2 of chart 1, sm, k1 (selvage st).
Cont in this way through row 23, removing markers on final (WS) row. Cut B.

SECOND STRIPE AND SHEEP
Join A.
Row 1 (RS) With A, sl 1 st, k51, pm, work row 1 of chart 2, pm, k to last st, k1.
Row 2 (WS) Sl 1 st, p to marker, sm, work row 2 of chart 2, sm, p to last st, k1.
Cont in this way through row 23, removing markers on final (RS) row. Cut A.

THIRD STRIPE AND SHEEP
Join B.
Row 1 (WS) With B, sl 1 st, p34, pm, work row 1 of chart 1, pm, p to last st, k1.
Row 2 (RS) Sl 1 st, k to marker, sm, work row 2 of chart 1, sm, k to last st, k1.
Cont in this way through row 23, working body of sheep in A and removing markers

Gauge
18 sts and 26 rows to 4"/10cm over St st using size 8 (5mm) needles.
Take time to check gauge.

Sleepy Sheep

on final (WS) row.
Cut B.

FOURTH STRIPE AND SHEEP
Join A.
Row 1 (RS) With A, sl 1 st, k17, pm, work row 1 of chart 2, pm, k to last st, k1.
Row 2 (WS) Sl 1 st, p to marker, sm, work row 2 of chart 2, sm, p to last st, k1.
Cont in this way through row 23, removing markers on final (RS) row.
Cut A.

FIFTH STRIPE AND SHEEP
Join B.
Row 1 (WS) With B, sl 1 st, p68, pm, work row 1 of chart 1, k1.
Row 2 (RS) Sl 1 st, work row 2 of chart 1, sm, k to last st, k1.
Cont in this way through row 23, removing markers on final (WS) row.
Cut B.

TOP BORDER
Join A.
Next row (RS) Sl 1 st, k to last st, k1.
Next row (WS) Beg with row 2 and cont selvage sts, work approx 2"/5cm of double seed st pat.
Bind off in pat.

SIDE BORDERS
With RS facing and A, pick up and k 105 sts evenly along side edge.
Work approx 2"/5cm in double seed st pat.
Bind off in pat.
Rep for other side border.

Finishing
Weave in ends.
Block to measurements. ∎

COLOR KEY
- ▨ (A)
- ☐ (B)
- ▨ (C)

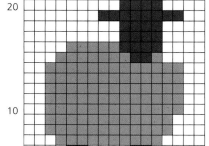

CHART 1

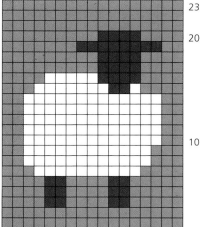

CHART 2

23
20

10

(WS) 1

17 sts

23
20

10

1

17 sts

Blissful Basketweave

This basketweave stitch pattern looks intricate
—but is made entirely of knit and purl stitches!

DESIGNED BY FELICITY THOMAS

Knitted Measurements
Approx 26 x 40"/66 x 101.5cm

Materials
▪ 5 3½oz/100g hanks (each approx 128yd/117m) of Cascade Yarns *128 Superwash* (superwash merino wool) in #231 Blue Mist ⑤
▪ One size 10 (6mm) circular needle, 40"/100cm long, *or size to obtain gauge*

Notes
1) Basketweave pat may be worked from text or chart.
2) Three edge stitches on each side are worked in garter stitch.
3) Circular needle is used to accommodate large number of stitches. Do *not* join.

Basketweave Pattern
(over a multiple of 12 sts plus 6)
Row 1 (RS) K3, *k4, p5, k1, p1, k1; rep from * to last 3 sts, k3.
Row 2 (WS) K3, *p1, k1, p1, k5, p4; rep from * to last 3 sts, k3.

Row 3 K3, *k5, p3, k3, p1; rep from * to last 3 sts, k3.
Row 4 K3, *k1, p3, k3, p5; rep from * to last 3 sts, k3.

Row 5 K3, *[p1, k5] twice; rep from * to last 3 sts, k3.
Row 6 K3, *[p5, k1] twice; rep from * to last 3 sts, k3.
Row 7 K3, *p2, k3, p1, k5, p1; rep from * to last 3 sts, k3.
Row 8 K3, *k1, p5, k1, p3, k2; rep from * to last 3 sts, k3.
Row 9 K3, *p3, k1, p1, k5, p2; rep from * to last 3 sts, k3.
Row 10 K3, *k2, p5, k1, p1, k3; rep from * to last 3 sts, k3.
Row 11 K3, *p4, k5, p3; rep from * to last 3 sts, k3.
Row 12 K3, *k3, p5, k4; rep from * to last 3 sts, k3.
Row 13 K3, *p3, k5, p1, k1, p2; rep from * to last 3 sts, k3.
Row 14 K3, *k2, p1, k1, p5, k3; rep from * to last 3 sts, k3.
Row 15 K3, *p2, k5, p1, k3, p1; rep from * to last 3 sts, k3.
Row 16 K3, *k1, p3, k1, p5, k2; rep from * to last 3 sts, k3.
Row 17 K3, *[p1, k5] twice; rep from * to last 3 sts, k3.

Gauge
16 sts and 22 rows to 4"/10cm over basketweave pattern using size 10 (6mm) needles.
Take time to check gauge.

Blissful Basketweave

Row 18 K3, *[p5, k1] twice; rep from * to last 3 sts, k3.

Row 19 K3, *k1, p1, k3, p3, k4; rep from * to last 3 sts, k3.

Row 20 K3, *p4, k3, p3, k1, p1; rep from * to last 3 sts, k3.

Row 21 K3, *k2, p1, k1, p5, k3; rep from * to last 3 sts, k3.

Row 22 K3, *p3, k5, p1, k1, p2; rep from * to last 3 sts, k3.

Row 23 K3, *k3, p7, k2; rep from * to last 3 sts, k3.

Row 24 K3, *p2, k7, p3; rep from * to last 3 sts, k3.

Rep rows 1–24 for basketweave pat.

Blanket

Cast on 102 sts.
Knit 6 rows.
Work rows 1–24 of basketweave pat 8 times.
Knit 6 rows.
Bind off.

Finishing

Weave in ends.
Block to measurements. ∎

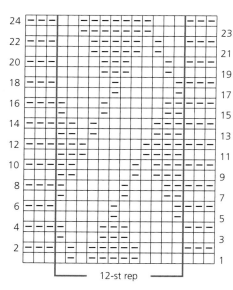

12-st rep

STITCH KEY

☐ k on RS, p on WS

⊟ p on RS, k on WS

Baby Ladybug

Ladybugs symbolize good luck, and any tot who gets to snuggle
under this adorable intarsia blanket is lucky, indeed.

DESIGNED BY LIDIA KARABINECH

Knitted Measurements
Approx 33 x 29½"/84 x 75cm

Materials
▨ 4 3½oz/100g hanks (each approx
150yd/137.5m) of Cascade Yarns *220
Superwash Aran* (superwash merino wool)
in #817 Aran (A) (4️⃣)
▨ 1 hank each in #893 Ruby (B) and
#815 Black (C)
▨ One size 8 (5mm) circular needle,
32"/80 cm long, *or size to obtain gauge*
▨ Stitch markers

Notes
1) Use a separate bobbin of yarn for each
color section. Do *not* carry yarn across
back of work.
2) When changing colors, twist yarns on
WS to prevent holes in work.
3) Blanket and chart are worked in St st
(k on RS, p on WS) with 5 sts worked in
seed st on each end for side borders.

Seed Stitch
(over an odd number of sts)
Row 1 K1,*p1, k1; rep from * to end.
Row 2 P the knit sts and k the purl sts.
Rep row 2 for seed st.

Blanket
With A, cast on 125 sts.

BOTTOM BORDER
Work in seed st for 10 rows.

BEGIN CHART
Row 1 (RS) Work 5 sts in seed st, pm,
k5, pm, work 60 sts in chart pat, pm,
k50, pm, work 5 sts in seed st.
Row 2 (WS) Work 5 sts in seed st, sm,
p50, sm, work 60 sts in chart pat, sm,
p5, sm, work 5 sts in seed st.
Work as established until row 75 of chart
has been worked. Cut B and C.
Next row (WS) With A, work 5 sts in
seed st, p to last 5 sts, removing chart
markers, work 5 sts in seed st.
Cont even in seed st and St st with A until
blanket measures 28"/71cm from beg.

TOP BORDER
Work in seed st for 10 rows.

Finishing
Weave in ends. Block to measurements. ∎

Gauge
15 sts and 22 rows to 4"/10cm over St st using size 8 (5mm) needles.
Take time to check gauge

18
Baby Ladybug

COLOR KEY

☐	A
■	B
■	C

75
70

60

50

40

30

20

10

1

60 sts

Happy Hearts

The lace-shaped heart motifs on this blanket, worked diagonally
from corner to corner, will show just how much you love the recipient.

DESIGNED BY CLEO MALONE

Knitted Measurements
Approx 23 x 23"/58.5 x 58.5cm

Materials
▪ 3 3½oz/100g hanks (each approx
150yd/137.5m) of Cascade Yarns *220
Superwash Aran* (superwash merino
wool) in #817 Aran ⬛④⬛
▪ One size 10 (6mm) circular needle,
24"/60cm or longer, *or size to obtain gauge*

Notes
1) This blanket is worked diagonally from
one point to opposite point, increasing
to full width, then decreasing back to
original number of cast-on stitches.
2) Lace pattern is given in charted format only.

Blanket
Cast on 3 sts.
Row 1 (RS) Kfb, k to end—4 sts.
Rows 2 and 3 Rep row 1 twice more—6 sts.
Row 4 (WS) Kfb, k1, p1, k3—7 sts.
Row 5 Kfb, k to end—8 sts.
Row 6 Kfb, k1, p3, k3—9 sts.
Row 7 Kfb, k to end—10 sts.
Row 8 Kfb, k1, p to last 3 sts, k3—11 sts.
Rows 9 and 10 Rep rows 7 and 8 once
more—13 sts.

FIRST MOTIF BAND
Row 11 Kfb, k4, work row 1 of chart A
over next 3 sts, k to end—14 sts.
Row 12 Kfb, k1, p to last 3 sts, k3—15 sts.
Row 13 Kfb, k4, work row 3 of chart A
over next 5 sts, k to end—16 sts.
Rows 14–23 Rep rows 12 and 13 five
times more, working chart A rows 4–13,
with 2 additional sts in pat as shown on
chart each RS row—26 sts.
Row 24 and all WS rows thru row 106
Kfb, k1, p to last 3 sts, k3—1 st inc'd.

Row 25 Kfb, k5, work row 15 of chart A
over next 15 sts, k to end—30 sts.
Row 27 Kfb, k6, work row 17 of chart A
over next 17 sts, k to end—32 sts.
Row 29 Kfb, k8, work row 19 of chart A
over next 15 sts, k to end—34 sts.

SECOND MOTIF BAND
Row 31 Kfb, k to end—36 sts.
Row 33 Kfb, k4, work row 1 of chart A
over next 3 sts, k21, work row 1 of chart
A over next 3 sts, k to end—38 sts.
Row 35 Kfb, k4, work row 3 of chart A
over next 5 sts, k19, work row 3 of chart
A over next 5 sts, k to end—40 sts.
Row 37 Kfb, k4, work row 5 of chart A
over next 7 sts, k17, work row 5 of chart
A over next 7 sts, k to end—42 sts.
Row 39 Kfb, k4, work row 7 of chart A
over next 9 sts, k15, work row 7 of chart
A over next 9 sts, k to end—44 sts.
Row 41 Kfb, k4, work row 9 of chart A
over next 11 sts, k13, work row 9 of chart
A over next 11 sts, k to end—46 sts.
Row 43 Kfb, k4, work row 11 of chart
A over next 13 sts, k11, work row 11 of
chart A over next 13 sts, k to end—48 sts.
Row 45 Kfb, k4, work row 13 of chart A
over next 15 sts, k9, work row 13 of chart

Gauge
16 sts and 25 rows to 4"/10cm over St st using size 10 (6mm) needles.
Take time to check gauge.

A over next 15 sts, k to end—50 sts.

Row 47 Kfb, k5, work row 15 of chart A over next 15 sts, k9, work row 15 of chart A over next 15 sts, k to end—56 sts.

Row 49 Kfb, k5, work row 17 of chart A over next 17 sts, k9, work row 17 of chart A over next 17 sts, k to end—58 sts.

Row 51 Kfb, k7, work row 19 of chart A over next 15 sts, k11, work row 19 of chart A over next 15 sts, k to end—60 sts.

THIRD MOTIF BAND

Row 53 Kfb, k to end— 62 sts.

Row 55 Kfb, k4, [work row 1 of chart A over next 3 sts, k22] twice, work row 1 of chart A over next 3 sts, k to end— 64 sts.

Row 57 Kfb, k4, [work row 3 of chart A over next 5 sts, k20] twice, work row 3 of chart A over next 5 sts, k to end—66 sts.

Row 59 Kfb, k4, [work row 5 of chart A over next 7 sts, k18] twice, work row 5 of chart A over next 7 sts, k to end—68 sts.

Row 61 Kfb, k4, [work row 7 of chart A over next 9 sts, k16] twice, work row 7 of chart A over next 9 sts, k to end—70 sts.

Row 63 Kfb, k4, [work row 9 of chart A over next 11 sts, k14] twice, work row 9 of chart A over next 11 sts, k to end—72 sts.

Row 65 Kfb, k4, [work row 11 of chart A over next 13 sts, k12] twice, work row 11 of chart A over next 13 sts, k to end—74 sts.

Row 67 Kfb, k4, [work row 13 of chart A over next 15 sts, k10] twice, work row 13 of chart A over next 15 sts, k to end—76 sts.

Row 69 Kfb, k5, [work row 15 of chart A over next 15 sts, k10] twice, work row 15 of chart A over next 15 sts, k to end—84 sts.

Row 71 Kfb, k6, [work row 17 of chart A over next 17 sts, k10] twice, work row 17 of chart A over next 17 sts, k to end—86 sts.

Row 73 Kfb, k8, [work row 19 of chart A

over next 15 sts, k12] twice, work row 19 of chart A over next 15 sts, k to end—88 sts.

FOURTH MOTIF BAND

Row 75 Kfb, k to end—90 sts.

Row 77 Kfb, k4, [work row 1 of chart A over next 3 sts, k23] 3 times, work row 1 of chart A over next 3 sts, k to end—92 sts.

Row 79 Kfb, k4, [work row 3 of chart A over next 5 sts, k21] 3 times, work row 3 of chart A over next 5 sts, k to end—94 sts.

Row 81 Kfb, k4, [work row 5 of chart A over next 7 sts, k19] 3 times, work row 5 of chart A over next 7 sts, k to end—96 sts.

Row 83 Kfb, k4, [work row 7 of chart A over next 9 sts, k17] 3 times, work row 7 of chart A over next 9 sts, k to end— 98 sts.

Row 85 Kfb, k4, [work row 9 of chart A over next 11 sts, k15] 3 times, work row 9 of chart A over next 11 sts, k to end—100 sts.

Row 87 Kfb, k4, [work row 11 of chart A over next 13 sts, k13] 3 times, work row 11 of chart A over next 13 sts, k to end—102 sts.

Row 89 Kfb, k4, [work row 13 of chart A over next 15 sts, k11] 3 times, work row 13 of chart A over next 15 sts, k to end—104 sts.

Row 91 Kfb, k5, [work row 15 of chart A over next 15 sts, k11] 3 times, work row 15 of chart A over next 15 sts, k to end—114 sts.

Row 93 Kfb, k6, [work row 17 of chart A over next 17 sts, k11] 3 times, work row 17 of chart A over next 17 sts, k to end—116 sts.

Row 95 Kfb, k8, [work row 19 of chart A over next 15 sts, k13] 3 times, work row 19 of chart A over next 15 sts, k to end—118 sts.

Row 97 Kfb, k to end—120 sts.

FIFTH MOTIF BAND

Row 99 Kfb, k30, work row 1 of chart A over next 3 sts, k19, work row 1 of chart B over next 15 sts, k19, work row 1 of chart A over next 3 sts, k to end—122 sts.

Row 101 Kfb, k30, work row 3 of chart A over next 5 sts, k17, work row 3 of chart B over next 17 sts, k17, work row 3 of chart A over next 5 sts, k to end—124 sts.

Row 103 Kfb, k30, work row 5 of chart A over next 7 sts, k16, work row 5 of chart B over next 17 sts, k16, work row 5 of chart A over next 7 sts, k to end—124 sts.

Row 105 Kfb, k30, work row 7 of chart A over next 9 sts, k15, work row 7 of chart B over next 15 sts, k15, work row 7 of chart A over next 9 sts, k to end—126 sts.

Row 107 Kfb, k30, work row 9 of chart A over next 11 sts, k16, work row 9 of chart B over next 11 sts, k16, work row 9 of chart A over next 11 sts, k to end— 128 sts.

Row 108 Kfb, k2, p to last 4 sts, k4— 129 sts.

Row 109 Ssk, k29, work row 11 of chart A over next 13 sts, k16, work row 11 of chart B over next 9 sts, k16, work row 11 of chart A over next 13 sts, k to end— 128 sts.

Row 110 and all WS rows thru row 208 Ssk, k2, p to last 4 sts, k4—1 st dec'd.

Row 111 Ssk, k27, work row 13 of chart A over next 15 sts, k16, work row 13 of chart B over next 7 sts, k16, work row 13 of chart A over next 15 sts, k to end—126 sts.

Row 113 Ssk, k26, work row 15 of chart A over next 15 sts, k17, work row 15 of chart B over next 5 sts, k17, work row 15 of chart

Happy Hearts

A over next 15 sts, k to end—128 sts.
Row 115 Ssk, k25, work row 17 of chart A over next 17 sts, k18, work row 17 of chart B over next 3 sts, k18, work row 17 of chart A of next 17 sts, k to end—126 sts.
Row 117 Ssk, k25, work row 19 of chart A over next 15 sts, k19, work row 13 of chart B over next 3 sts, k19, work row 19 of chart A over next 15 sts, k to end—124 sts.
Row 119 Ssk, k to end—122 sts.

SIXTH MOTIF BAND
Row 121 Ssk, k8, [work row 1 of chart B over next 15 sts, k14] 3 times, work row 1 of chart B over next 15 sts, k to end—120 sts.
Row 123 Ssk, k6, [work row 3 of chart B over next 17 sts, k12] 3 times, work row 3 of chart B over next 17 sts, k to end—118 sts.
Row 125 Ssk, k5, [work row 5 of chart B over next 17 sts, k12] 3 times, work row 5 of chart B over next 17 sts, k to end—108 sts.
Row 127 Ssk, k4, [work row 7 of chart B over next 15 sts, k12] 3 times, work row 7 of chart B over next 15 sts, k to

end—106 sts.
Row 129 Ssk, k5, [work row 9 of chart B over next 11 sts, k16] 3 times, work row 9 of chart B over next 11 sts, k to end—104 sts.
Row 131 Ssk, k5, [work row 11 of chart B over next 9 sts, k18] 3 times, work row 11 of chart B over next 9 sts, k to end—102 sts.
Row 133 Ssk, k5, [work row 13 of chart B over next 7 sts, k20] 3 times, work row 13 of chart B over next 7 sts, k to end—100 sts.
Row 135 Ssk, k5, [work row 15 of chart B over next 5 sts, k22] 3 times, work row 15 of chart B over next 5 sts, k to end—98 sts.
Row 137 Ssk, k5, [work row 17 of chart B over next 3 sts, k24] 3 times, work row 17 of chart B over next 5 sts, k to end—96 sts.
Row 139 Ssk, k4, [work row 19 of chart B over next 3 sts, k24] 3 times, work row 19 of chart B over next 3 sts, k to end—94 sts.
Row 141 Ssk, k to end—92 sts.

SEVENTH MOTIF BAND
Row 143 Ssk, k11, [work row 1 of chart B over next 15 sts, k11] twice, work row 1 of chart B over next 15 sts, k to end—90 sts.
Row 145 Ssk, k9, [work row 3 of chart B

over next 17 sts, k9] twice, work row 3 of chart B over next 17 sts, k to end—88 sts.
Row 147 Ssk, k8, [work row 5 of chart B over next 17 sts, k9] twice, work row 5 of chart B over next 17 sts, k to end—80 sts.
Row 149 Ssk, k7, [work row 7 of chart B over next 15 sts, k9] twice, work row 7 of chart B over next 15 sts, k to end—78 sts.
Row 151 Ssk, k8, [work row 9 of chart B over next 11 sts, k13] twice, work row 9 of chart B over next 11 sts, k to end—76 sts.
Row 153 Ssk, k8, [work row 11 of chart B over next 9 sts, k15] twice, work row 11 of chart B over next 9 sts, k to end—74 sts.
Row 155 Ssk, k8, [work row 13 of chart B over next 7 sts, k17] twice, work row 13 of chart B over next 7 sts, k to end—72 sts.
Row 157 Ssk, k8, [work row 15 of chart B over next 5 sts, k19] twice, work row 15 of chart B over next 5 sts, k to end—70 sts.
Row 159 Ssk, k8, [work row 17 of chart B over next 3 sts, k21] twice, work row 17 of chart B over next 3 sts, k to end—68 sts.

CHART A

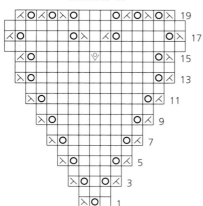

CHART B

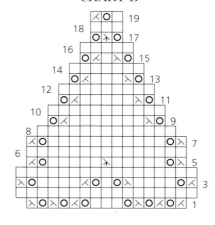

STITCH KEY

☐ k on RS, p on WS

⊠ k2tog

⊠ ssk

⊼ SK2P

◯ yo

▽ (k1, yo, k1) in same st

Row 161 Ssk, k7, [work row 19 of chart B over next 3 sts, k21] twice, work row 19 of chart B over next 3 sts, k to end—66 sts.
Row 163 Ssk, k to end—64 sts.

EIGHTH MOTIF BAND
Row 165 Ssk, k10, work row 1 of chart B over next 15 sts, k10, work row 1 of chart B over next 15 sts, k to end—62 sts.
Row 167 Ssk, k8, work row 3 of chart B over next 17 sts, k8, work row 3 of chart B over next 17 sts, k to end—60 sts.
Row 169 Ssk, [k8, work row 5 of chart B over next 17 sts] twice, k to end—54 sts.
Row 171 Ssk, k7, work row 7 of chart B over next 15 sts, k8, work row 7 of chart B over next 15 sts, k to end—52 sts.
Row 173 Ssk, k8, work row 9 of chart B over next 11 sts, k12, work row 9 of chart B over next 11 sts, k to end—50 sts.
Row 175 Ssk, k8, work row 11 of chart B over next 9 sts, k14, work row 11 of chart B over next 9 sts, k to end—48 sts.
Row 177 Ssk, k8, work row 13 of chart B over next 7 sts, k16, work row 13 of chart B over next 7 sts, k to end—46 sts.
Row 179 Ssk, k8, work row 15 of chart B over next 5 sts, k18, work row 15 of chart B over next 5 sts, k to end—44 sts.
Row 181 Ssk, k8, work row 17 of chart B over next 3 sts, k20, work row 17 of chart B over next 3 sts, k to end—42 sts.
Row 183 Ssk, k7, work row 19 of chart B over next 3 sts, k20, work row 19 of chart B over next 3 sts, k to end—40 sts.
Row 185 Ssk, k to end—38 sts.

NINTH MOTIF BAND
Row 187 Ssk, k10, work row 1 of chart B over next 15 sts, k to end—36 sts.
Row 189 Ssk, k8, work row 3 of chart B over next 17 sts, k to end—34 sts.
Row 191 Ssk, k8, work row 5 of chart B

over next 17 sts, k to end—30 sts.
Row 193 Ssk, k7, work row 7 of chart B over next 15 sts, k to end—28 sts.
Row 195 Ssk, k8, work row 9 of chart B over next 11 sts, k to end—26 sts.
Row 197 Ssk, k8, work row 11 of chart B over next 9 sts, k to end—24 sts.
Row 199 Ssk, k8, work row 13 of chart B over next 7 sts, k to end—22 sts.
Row 201 Ssk, k8, work row 15 of chart B over next 5 sts, k to end—20 sts.
Row 203 Ssk, k8, work row 17 of chart B over next 3 sts, k to end—18 sts.
Row 205 Ssk, k7, work row 19 of chart B over next 3 sts, k to end—16 sts.

Row 207 Ssk, k to end—14 sts.
Row 209 Ssk, k to last 2 sts, k2tog—11 sts.
Row 210 Ssk, k2, p5, k2, k2tog—9 sts.
Row 211 Ssk, k to last 2 sts, k2tog—7 sts.
Rows 212 and 213 Rep row 211 twice more—3 sts.
Row 214 K2tog, k1, pass first st over 2nd st—1 st.
Cut yarn and fasten off rem st.

Finishing
Weave in ends.
Block to measurements. ∎

20 Watermelon Slice

This whimsical blanket is as fresh, colorful, and juicy as the fruit that inspired it!

DESIGNED BY GRACE VERDEROSA

Knitted Measurements
Approx 26½ x 24"/67.5 x 61cm

Materials
- 1 3½oz/100g skein (each approx 220yd/200m) of Cascade Yarns *220 Superwash Merino* (superwash merino wool) each in #10 Dark Moss (A) and #13 Lime (B) (4)
- 3 skeins in #23 Azalea Pink (C)
- Small amount in #28 Black (D)
- One size 7 (4.5mm) circular needle, 40"/100cm long, *or size to obtain gauge*
- Stitch markers
- Tapestry needle

Note
Circular needle is used to accommodate large number of stitches. Do *not* join.

Blanket
With A, cast on 125 sts.
Row 1 (RS) K1, *p1, k1; rep from * to end.

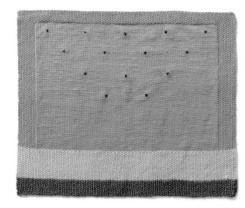

Row 2 K the purl sts and p the knit sts. Rep row 2 for seed st until piece measures 2"/5cm from beg. Change to B and cont in seed st until piece measures 5½"/14cm from beg.
Change to C and work as foll:

Row 1 (RS) K1, *p1, k1; rep from * to end.
Row 2 (WS) K1, [p1, k1] 5 times, pm, p to last 11 sts, pm, k1, [p1, k1] 5 times.
Row 3 K1, [p1, k1] 5 times, sm, k to marker, sm, k1, [p1, k1] 5 times.
Row 4 K1, [p1, k1] 5 times, sm, p to marker, sm, k1, [p1, k1] 5 times.
Rep rows 3 and 4 until piece measures 22"/56cm from beg, end with a WS row.
Cont with C, work in seed st over all sts for 2"/5cm.
Bind off loosely in pat.

Finishing
With D, work watermelon seed details using duplicate st (see page 182) as foll: Work a row of 5 seeds 2½"/6.5cm from top, a row of 4 seeds 5"/12.5cm from top, a row of 3 seeds 8"/20.5cm from top, and a row of 2 seeds 11"/28cm, spacing evenly and using photo as guide.
Weave in ends.
Block to measurements. ■

Gauge
20 sts and 28 rows to 4"/10cm over St st using size 7 (4.5mm) needle.
Take time to check gauge.

Railroad Tracks

Texture—created by alternating rows of garter stitch—takes center stage in this striking blanket, while an orange I-cord frame gives a bold finish.

DESIGNED BY CHERYL LAVENHAR

Knitted Measurements
Approx 25 x 25"/63.5 x 63.5cm

Materials
■ 2 3½oz/100g balls (each approx 220yd/200m) of Cascade Yarns *220 Superwash* (superwash wool) each in #892 Space Needle (A) and #817 Aran (B) ⓷
■ 1 ball in #907 Tangerine Heather (C)
■ Size 6 (4mm) circular needle, 24"/60cm long, *or size to obtain gauge*
■ One size 6 (4mm) double-pointed needle (dpn)
■ Stitch markers

Note
Circular needle is used to accommodate large number of sts. Do *not* join.

Blanket
With circular needle and A, cast on 120 sts.
Rows 1 and 2 With B, k8, *p8, k8; rep from * to end.
Rows 3 and 4 With A, k8, *p8, k8; rep from * to end.

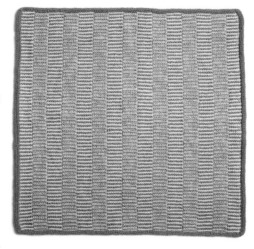

Rep rows 1–4 until piece measures approx 25"/63.5cm from beg, end with a row 2 of pat. With A, bind off.

I-CORD EDGING
With RS facing and C, pick up and k 1 st in every st along top, pm, pick up and k 1 st for every garter ridge along left side, pm, pick up and k 1 st in every st along bottom, pm, pick up and k 1 st for every garter ridge along right side, pm.
Cast on 4 sts to LH needle.
*Next row (RS) Using dpn, k3, k2tog tbl, sl 4 sts back to LH needle, pull yarn snug across back of work.
Rep last row and work across sts to next marker.
Turn work.
Corner row (WS) P4. Turn work.
Rep from * 3 times more, removing markers. Turn work and bind off rem sts purlwise.
Sew ends of I-cord tog.

Finishing
Weave in ends.
Block to measurements. ■

Gauge
19 sts and 42 rows to 4"/10cm over garter st using size 6 (4mm) needle.
Take time to check gauge.

22 Southwest Starburst

Adobe red and turquoise, along with a tribal-style motif, give this vivid blanket a generous helping of Southwestern style.

DESIGNED BY AMY MICALLEF

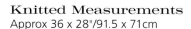

Knitted Measurements
Approx 36 x 28"/91.5 x 71cm

Materials
- 1 3½oz/100g ball (approx 220yd/200m) of Cascade Yarns *220 Superwash* (superwash wool) in #808 Sunset Orange (A)
- 3 balls in #815 Black (B)
- 2 balls each in #817 Aran (C), #812 Turquoise (D), and #1973 Seafoam Heather (E)
- Size 7 (4.5mm) circular needle, 40"/100cm long, *or size to obtain gauge*
- Bobbins

Notes
1) Use a separate bobbin of yarn for each color section. Do *not* carry yarn across back of work.
2) When changing colors, twist yarns on WS to prevent holes in work.
3) One selvedge st is worked on each side in same color as edge st of chart.
4) Charts are worked in St st (k on RS, p on WS).
5) Circular needle is used to accommodate large number of stitches. Do *not* join.

Blanket
With D, cast on 36 sts; with B, cast on 82 sts; with D, cast on 36 sts—154 sts.

BEGIN CHARTS 1 AND 2
Row 1 (RS) With D, k1 (selvage st); work chart 1 over 76 sts, work chart 2 over 76 sts; with D, k1 (selvage st).
Row 2 With D, k1; work chart 2 as established, work chart 1 as established; with D, k1.
Working selvage sts in garter st (k every row) and in same color as edge st of chart row, cont to work charts in this way through row 86.

BEGIN CHARTS 3 AND 4
Row 87 (RS) With E, k1; work chart 3 over 76 sts, work chart 4 over 76 sts; with E, k1.
Row 88 With E, k1; work chart 4 as established, work chart 3 as established; with E, k1.
Working selvage sts in garter st, cont to work charts in this way through row 170.
Row 171 Bind off using color shown in last chart row.

Finishing
SIDE EDGES (MAKE 2)
With B, cast on 13 sts.
Row 1 (WS) Sl 1, k1, p10, k1.
Row 2 (RS) K11, p1, k1.
Rep rows 1 and 2 until edge fits along

Gauge
20 sts and 26 rows to 4"/10cm over St st using size 7 (4.5mm) needle.
Take time to check gauge

Southwest Starburst

side edge of blanket. Bind off.
Sew edge to side edge of blanket.
Rep for other side edge.

TOP AND BOTTOM EDGES (MAKE 2)
Work as for side edges until edge fits
along top edge of blanket, including

side edges. Do *not* bind off. Sew edge to
top edge of blanket, adding extra rows, if
necessary, to fit smoothly.
Bind off. Rep for bottom edge.

Weave in ends.
Block to measurements. ■

CHART 2

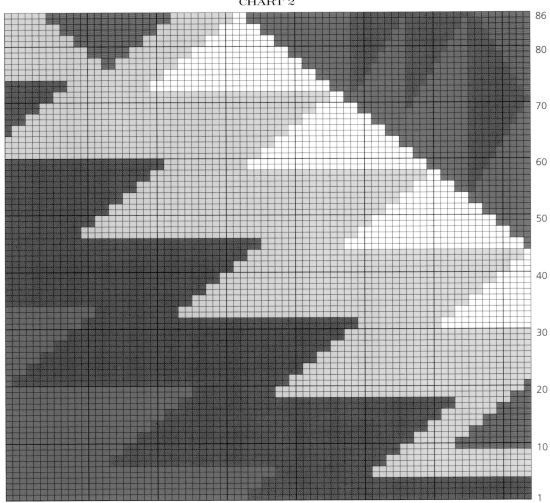

76 sts

CHART 1

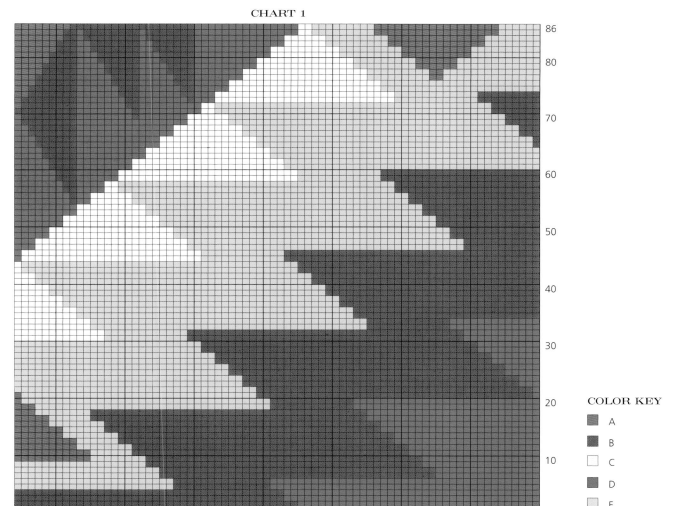

COLOR KEY

- A
- B
- C
- D
- E

76 sts

71

Southwest Starburst

CHART 4

76 sts

CHART 3

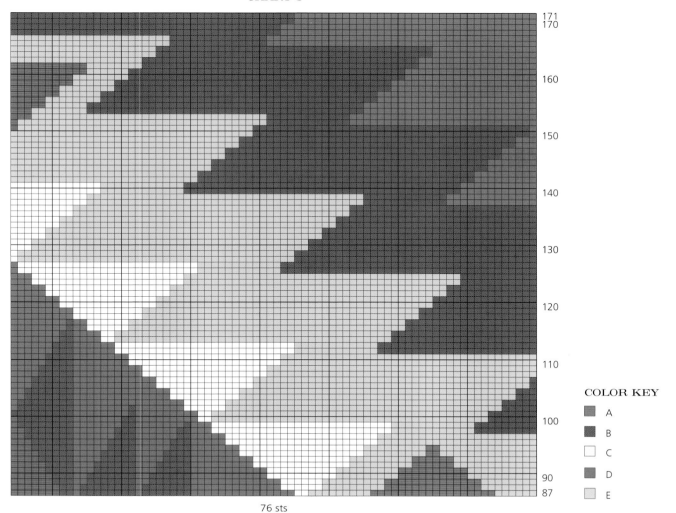

171
170

160

150

140

130

120

110

100

90
87

76 sts

COLOR KEY

A
B
C
D
E

73

23

Lacy Leaves

Leaf-shaped lace motifs arrayed in diamond frames create a lovely blanket that will be treasured for years to come.

DESIGNED BY YOKO HATTA

Knitted Measurements
Approx 23 x 24"/58.5 x 61cm

Materials
■ 3 3½oz/100g skeins (each approx 220yd/200m) of Cascade Yarns *220 Superwash Merino* (superwash merino wool) in #30 Sugar Coral ③
■ One each sizes 5 and 7 (3.75 and 4.5mm) circular needles, 40"/100cm long *or size to obtain gauge*
■ Stitch markers

Note
Circular needle is used to accommodate large number of stitches. Do *not* join.

Blanket
With smaller needle, cast on 121 sts. Work 10 rows in garter st (k every row). Change to larger needle.

BEGIN CHART
Row 1 (RS) K5, pm, work to rep line, work 10-st rep 10 times, work to end of chart, pm, k5.
Row 2 K5, sm, work chart as established to marker, sm, k5.
Working 5 sts each side in garter st, cont to work chart in this way until 16 rows of chart have been worked 10 times. Remove markers.
Work 10 rows in garter st. Bind off.

Finishing
Weave in ends.
Block to measurements. ■

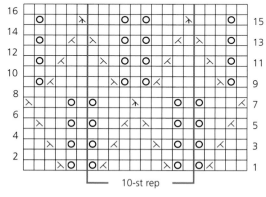

10-st rep

STITCH KEY
☐ k on RS, p on WS
― p on RS, k on WS
Ⓞ yo
╱ k2tog
╲ ssk
⋏ SK2P

Gauge
21 sts and 29 rows to 4"/10cm over chart using size 7 (4.5mm) needle.
Take time to check gauge.

Over the Rainbow

Chasing rainbows is a pleasure with this crayon-bright motif,
knit in sections using separate miniballs of each contrast color. Pot of gold not included!

DESIGNED BY AUDREY DRYSDALE

Knitted Measurements
Approx 31 x 29½"/79 x 75cm

Materials
■ 3 3½oz/100g hanks (each approx 150yd/137.5m) of Cascade Yarns *220 Superwash Aran* (superwash merino wool) in #875 Feather Grey (A) (4)
■ 1 hank each in #249 Amethyst (B), #1999 Majolica Blue (C), #849 Dark Aqua (D), #802 Green Apple (E), #241 Sunflower (F), #822 Pumpkin (G), and #809 Really Red (H)
■ One size 8 (5mm) circular needle, 29" (74cm) long, *or size to obtain gauge*
■ Stitch markers

Double Moss Stitch
(over a multiple of 4 sts plus 2)
Row 1 (RS) *P2, k2; rep from * to last 2 sts, p2.
Row 2 (WS) *K2, p2; rep from * to last 2 sts, k2.
Row 3 *K2, p2; rep from * to last 2 sts, k2.
Row 4 *P2, k2; rep from * to last 2 sts, p2.
Rep rows 1–4 for double moss st.

Notes
1) Wind two balls of each rainbow color and work each section separately without floating strands behind the piece. Cut the second strand of each rainbow color on the first row where the two halves of the rainbow meet. Use separate balls of A for the center under the arch, and the second side edge.

2) When changing colors, twist yarns on WS to prevent holes in work.
3) Circular needle is used to accommodate large number of stitches. Do *not* join.

Blanket
BOTTOM BORDER
With A, cast on 142 sts.
Work in double moss st for 14 rows, end with a WS row and inc 1 st at center of last row—143 sts.
Next row (RS) Work 12 sts in double moss st, pm, k to last 12 sts, pm, work to end in double moss st.
Next row (WS) Work 12 sts in double moss st, sm, p to last 12 sts, sm, work to end in double moss st.
Cont in pat until piece measures 6"/15cm from beg, end with a WS row.

BEGIN CHART
Row 1 (RS) Work 12 sts in double moss st, sm, work row 1 of chart (first half),

Gauge
18 sts and 27 rows to 4"/10cm in St st using size 8 (5mm) needles.
Take time to check gauge.

24

Over the Rainbow

work row 1 of chart (second half), sm, work 12 sts in double moss st.

Row 2 (WS) Work 12 sts in double moss st, sm, work row 2 of chart (second half), work row 1 of chart (first half), sm, work 12 sts in double moss st. Rep rows 1 and 2 thirteen times more for legs of rainbow.

Work rows 3 through 95 of charts, maintaining double moss st borders.

Cut H and cont with A only.

Next row (WS) Work 12 sts in double moss st, sm, p to marker, sm, work 12 sts in double moss st.

Next row (RS) Work 12 sts in double moss st, sm, k to marker, sm, work 12 sts in double moss st.

Cont in pat until piece measures 27½"/70cm from beg, end with a WS row, dec 1 st at center of last row—142 sts.

TOP BORDER
Work in double moss st over all sts for 13 rows.
Bind off all sts in pat.

Finishing
Weave in ends.
Block to measurements. ■

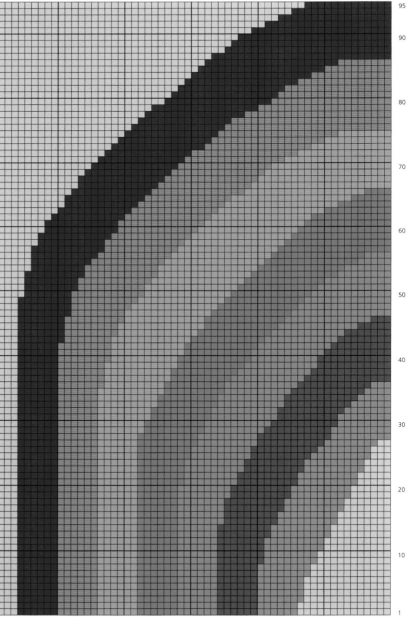

119   61

CHART (FIRST HALF)

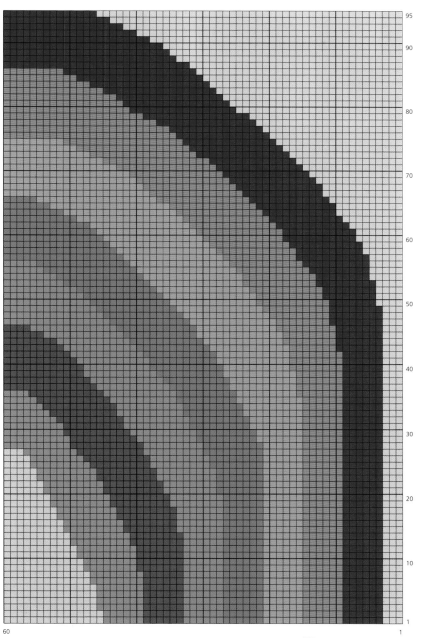

COLOR KEY

- A
- B
- C
- D
- E
- F
- G
- H

25

Slip-Stitch Sunshine

Shades of gray are right on trend,
while slip-stitch dots add sunshine to this gender-neutral classic.

DESIGNED BY CHERYL MURRAY

◗■☐☐

Knitted Measurements
Approx 13½ x 29"/34.5 x 73.5cm

Materials
▨ 2 3½oz/100g skeins (each approx 220yd/200m) of Cascade Yarns *220 Superwash Merino* (superwash merino wool) in #27 Charcoal (A) (🄲)
▨ 1 skein each in #09 Lemon (B) and #26 Silver Heather (C)
▨ One pair size 9 (5.5mm) needles, *or size to obtain gauge*
▨ One size 9 (5.5mm) circular needle, 40"/100cm long
▨ Stitch markers

Garter Slip-Stitch Stripe Pattern
(over an odd number of sts)
Rows 1 and 2 With A, knit.
Row 3 (RS) With B, k1, *sl 1 wyib, k1; rep from * to end.
Row 4 (WS) With B, k1, *sl 1 wyif, k1; rep from * to end.
Rows 5 and 6 With C, knit.
Row 7 With A, k1, *sl 1 wyib, k1; rep from * to end.
Row 8 With A, k1, *sl 1 wyif, k1; rep from * to end.
Rows 9 and 10 With B, knit.

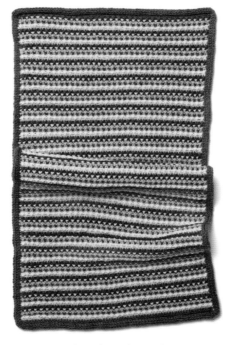

Row 11 With C, k1, *sl 1 wyib, k1; rep from * to end.
Row 12 With C, k1, *sl 1 wyif, k1; rep from * to end.
Rep rows 1–12 for garter sl-st stripe pat.

Blanket
With A, cast on 73 sts.
Work rows 1–12 of garter sl-st stripe pat until piece measures approx 28"/71cm from beg, end with row 2 of pat.
Bind off all sts knitwise.

Finishing
I-CORD EDGING
With A, circular needle, and RS facing, pick up and k 150 sts evenly along long edge of blanket, pm, 73 sts evenly along short edge, pm, 150 sts evenly along rem long edge, pm, and 73 sts evenly along rem short edge. Cast on 3 sts to LH side of circular needle—449 sts.
Do *not* turn.
Row 1 (RS) *[K2, ssk; without turning work, sl 3 sts back to LH needle] to corner marker, k3; without turning work, sl 3 sts back to LH needle; rep from * until all picked-up sts are worked—3 sts rem. Without turning work, sl sts back to opposite end of needle, k3.
Cut yarn.
Using tail, sew edges of I-cord tog.

Weave in ends.
Block to measurements. ∎

Gauge
22 sts and 44 rows to 4"/10cm over garter sl-st stripe pat using size 9 (5.5mm) needles.
Take time to check gauge.

26 Favorite T-Shirt

Baby's blanket is soft and cushy, with crisp stripes, just like Mom's or Dad's favorite t-shirt.

DESIGNED BY ANN REGIS

Knitted Measurements
Approx 24 x 34"/61 x 86.5cm

Materials
■ 3 3½oz/100g hanks (each approx 150yd/137.5m) of Cascade Yarns *220 Superwash Aran* (superwash merino wool) in #845 Denim (A) ④
■ 2 hanks in #817 Aran (B)
■ One size 9 (5.5mm) circular needle, 24"/60cm long, *or size to obtain gauge*
■ Stitch markers

Note
Circular needle is used to accommodate large number of sts. Do *not* join.

Blanket
With A, cast on 100 sts.

BOTTOM BORDER
Row 1 (RS) Knit.
Row 2 *[K3, p2] twice, k3, pm, [p2, k5] twice, p2, pm; rep from * twice more, [k3, p2] twice, k3.
Rep rows 1 and 2 four times more.
Knit 2 rows.

BEGIN STRIPES
Row 1 (RS) Knit.
Row 2 *[K3, p2] twice, k3, sm, p16, sm; rep from * twice more, [k3, p2] twice, k3.
Rep rows 1 and 2 in color sequence as foll:
28 rows A.
24 rows B.
16 rows A.
16 rows B.
16 rows A.
[4 rows B, 4 rows A] 5 times.
4 rows B.
8 rows A.
14 rows B.
12 rows A.

TOP BORDER
With A, knit 2 rows.
Row 1 (RS) Knit.
Row 2 *[K3, p2] twice, k3, [p2, k5] twice, p2; rep from * twice more, [k3, p2] twice, k3.
Rep rows 1 and 2 four times more.
Bind off knitwise.

Finishing
Weave in ends.
Block to measurements. ■

Gauge
16 sts and 24 rows to 4"/10cm over St st using size 9 (5.5mm) needle.
Take time to check gauge.

Graphic Glam

A striking post-modern motif is surprisingly easy to make;
just like a quilt, it's all in the placement of the identical blocks.

DESIGNED BY IRINA POLUDNENKO

Knitted Measurements
Approx 33 x 33"/84 x 84cm

Materials
■ 6 3½oz/100g hanks (each approx 150yd/137.5m) of Cascade Yarns *220 Superwash Aran* (superwash merino wool) in #1946 Silver Grey (A) ④
■ 2 hanks each in #817 Aran (B) and #900 Charcoal (C)
■ One pair size 8 (5mm) needles, *or size to obtain gauge*

Note
This blanket is made of 36 squares that are sewn together to form the graphic pattern.

Blanket
SMALL SQUARE (MAKE 36)
With B, cast on 1 st.
Row 1 (K1, yo, k1) in same st—3 sts.
Row 2 Knit.
Row 3 K1, (k1, p1, k1) in next st, k1—5 sts.
Row 4 Knit.
Row 5 K1, (k1, p1) in next st, k to last 2 sts, (k1, p1) in next st, k1—7 sts.

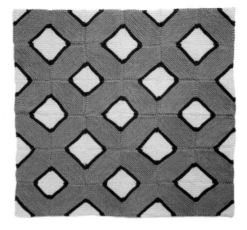

Row 6 Knit.
Rows 7–14 Rep rows 5 and 6 four times more—15 sts. Cut B.
Rows 15–18 With C, rep rows 5 and 6 twice more—19 sts. Cut C.
Rows 19–32 With A, rep rows 5 and 6 seven times more—33 sts.
Row 33 K1, ssk, k to last 3 sts, k2tog, k1—31 sts.
Row 34 Knit.
Rows 35–46 With A, rep rows 33 and

34 six times more—19 sts. Cut A.
Rows 47–50 With C, rep rows 33 and 34 twice more—15 sts. Cut C.
Rows 51–60 With B, rep rows 33 and 34 five times more—5 sts.
Row 61 K1, k3tog, k1—3 sts.
Row 62 Knit.
Row 63 K3tog.
Cut B and fasten off rem st.

Finishing
Sew 4 small squares tog foll assembly diagram below. Rep 8 times more for a total of 9 large squares.
Arrange 9 large squares into a 3x3 grid and sew tog.
Weave in ends.
Block to measurements. ■

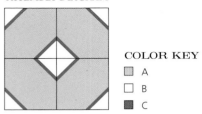

ASSEMBLY DIAGRAM

COLOR KEY
□ A
□ B
■ C

Gauge
17 sts and 33 rows to 4"/10cm over garter st using size 8 (5mm) needles.
Take time to check gauge.

Diamond Lace

A delightful lace pattern in sweet candy pink
is finished with a scalloped crochet edging.

DESIGNED BY ANASTASIA BLAES

Knitted Measurements
Approx 20½ x 30"/52 x 76cm

Materials
▨ 3 3½oz/100g balls (each approx
220yd/200m) of Cascade Yarns *220
Superwash* (superwash wool) in #894
Strawberry Cream (**3**)
▨ Size 7 (4.5mm) circular needle,
24"/60cm long, *or size to obtain gauge*
▨ One size 7 (4.5mm) crochet hook

Diamond Lace Pattern
(over a multiple of 8 sts plus 11)
Row 1 (RS) K3, *k3, k2tog, yo, k3; rep
from * to end.
Row 2 and all even-numbered rows
K3, p to last 3 sts, k3.
Row 3 K3, *k2, k2tog, yo, k1, yo, ssk, k1;
rep from * to last 8 sts, k2, k2tog, yo, k4.
Row 5 K3, *k1, k2tog, yo, k3, yo, ssk;
rep from * to last 8 sts, k1, k2tog, yo, k5.
Row 7 K3, *k3, yo, SK2P, yo, k2; rep
from * to last 8 sts, k3, yo, ssk, k3.
Row 9 K2, *k2tog, yo, k6; rep from * to
last 9 sts, k2tog, yo, k7.
Row 11 K3, *k1, yo, ssk, k3, k2tog, yo;

rep from * to last 8 sts, k1, yo, ssk, k5.
Row 13 K3, *k2, yo, ssk, k1, k2tog, yo,
k1; rep from * to last 8 sts, k2, yo, ssk, k4.
Row 15 K3, k2tog, yo, *k5, yo, SK2P, yo;

rep from * to last 6 sts, k6.
Row 16 K3, p to last 3 sts, end k3.
Rep rows 1–16 for diamond lace pat.

Notes
1) Diamond lace pattern can be worked
from either written instructions or chart.
2) Circular needle is used to
accommodate large number of sts.
Do *not* join.

Blanket
Cast on 99 sts.
Knit 6 rows.

BEGIN LACE PATTERN
Work rows 1–16 of diamond lace pat
until piece measures approx 29"/73.5cm
from beg, end with row 16.
Knit 6 rows.
Bind off all sts loosely knitwise.

CROCHETED LACE EDGING
With RS facing and crochet hook, sl st in
top right corner of blanket.
Rnd 1 Ch 1, *sc in each st to corner, ch 1,
sc in each garter ridge along side edge to

Gauge
20 sts and 35 rows to 4"/10cm over diamond lace pat using size 7 (4.5mm) needle.
Take time to check gauge.

Diamond Lace

corner, ch 1; rep from * once more, sl st to join end of rnd.

Rnd 2 Ch 1, *[skip next sc, 5 dc in next sc, skip next sc, sl st in next sc] to corner, work 5 dc in corner ch-1 sp; rep from * 3 times more, join with a sl st in beg ch. Fasten off.

Finishing
Weave in ends.
Block to measurements. ∎

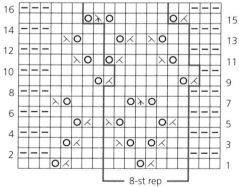

CHART

8-st rep

STITCH KEY

☐ k on RS, p on WS

– p on RS, k on WS

○ yo

╱ k2tog

╲ ssk

⅄ SK2P

Beautiful Borders

Knit in luxuriously soft merino wool,
this blanket is worked in two separate pieces and then grafted together.

DESIGNED BY JULIE TURJOMAN

Knitted Measurements
Approx 31 x 35½"/78.5 x 90cm

Materials
■ 4 3½oz/100g skeins (each approx 220yd/200m) of Cascade Yarns *220 Superwash Merino* (superwash merino wool) in #27 Charcoal (A) **③**
■ 1 skein in #30 Sugar Coral (B)
■ Two size 7 (4.5mm) circular needles, 24"/60cm long, *or size to obtain gauge*
■ One size 7 (4.5mm) circular needle, 32"/80cm long

K2, P2 Rib
(over a multiple of 4 sts plus 2)
Row 1 (RS) K2, *p2, k2; rep from * to end.
Row 2 (WS) P2, *k2, p2; rep from * to end.
Rep rows 1 and 2 for k2, p2 rib.

Two-Color Slip Stitch Pattern
(over a multiple of 4 sts plus 1)
Row 1 (WS) With A, purl.
Row 2 (RS) With B, k1, *sl 1 wyib, sl 1 wyif, sl 1 wyib, k1; rep from * to end.
Row 3 With B, p1, *sl 3 wyib, yo, p1; rep from * to end.

Row 4 With A, knit, dropping yo's.
Row 5 With A, purl.
Row 6 With B, k1, *sl 1 wyib, insert RH needle under loose strand from 2 rows below and knit tog with next st, sl 1 wyib, k1; rep from * to end.
Row 7 With B, p1, *sl 1 wyif, p1, sl 1 wyif, k1; rep from * to end.
Row 8 With A, knit.

Row 9 With A, purl.
Row 10 With B, k1, *sl 1 wyif, k1; rep from * to end.
Row 11 With B, purl.
Row 12 With A, k1, *sl 1 wyib, sl 1 wyif, sl 1 wyib, k1; rep from * to end.
Row 13 With A, p1, *sl 3 wyib, yo, p1; rep from * to end.
Row 14 With B, knit, dropping yo's.
Row 15 With B, purl.
Row 16 With A, k1, *sl 1 wyib, insert RH needle under loose strand from 2 rows below and knit tog with next st, sl 1 wyib, k1; rep from * to end.
Row 17 With A, p1, *sl 1 wyif, p1, sl 1 wyif, k1; rep from * to end.
Row 18 With B, knit.
Row 19 With B, purl.
Row 20 With A, k1, *sl 1 wyif, k1; rep from * to end.

Notes
1) Slip-stitch sections will have slightly tighter stitch and row gauge than St st section, due to slipped stitches and floats. These sections can be blocked to closely match St st gauge.
2) Blanket is worked in two pieces, which

Gauge
20 sts and 28 rows to 4"/10cm in St st using size 7 (4.5mm) needle.
Take time to check gauge.

Beautiful Borders

are joined by grafting.
Ribbed side borders are worked after grafting is done.
3) Slip all stitches purlwise.

Blanket
FIRST BORDER
With shorter needle and A, cast on 150 sts. Do *not* join.
Work in K2, P2 rib until piece measures approx 1"/2.5cm, end with a WS row.
Next row (RS) K75, k2tog, k to end—149 sts.

Begin slip-stitch section
Join B and work rows 1–20 of two-color sl-st pat, then work rows 1–11 again. Cut B.
Next row (RS) With A, knit.
Do *not* bind off. Cut A and set aside to be grafted later.

SECOND BORDER AND MAIN SECTION
With 2nd shorter needle, work as for first border. Cut B.
With A, work even in St st (k on RS, p on WS) until piece measures approx 31½"/80cm from beg.

Finishing
Lay both pieces on a flat surface with RS facing. With A, graft tog using Kitchener stitch (see page 182).

RIBBED SIDE BORDERS
With RS facing, longer circular needle, and A, pick up and k 186 sts evenly along side edge.
Begin on WS with a row 2, work in K2, P2 rib for 1"/2.5cm. Bind off all sts in pat. Rep along rem side edge.

Weave in ends
Block to measurements. ∎

30

Inverted Stripes

Flip the order of the contrasting stripes to mix things up a bit in this snuggly garter stitch cuddler.

DESIGNED BY LISA CRAIG

Knitted Measurements
Approx 22½ x 35¾"/57 x 91cm

Materials
■ 4 3½oz/100g hanks (each approx 150yd/137.5m) of Cascade Yarns *220 Superwash Aran* (superwash merino wool) in #1998 Aqua (A) ④
■ 1 hank each in #1946 Silver Grey (B) and #900 Charcoal (C)
■ One pair size 8 (5mm) needles, *or size to obtain gauge*

Blanket
With A, cast on 101 sts. Work in garter st (k every row) and stripe sequence as foll:
30 rows A.
4 rows B.
4 rows A.

4 rows B.
4 rows A.
4 rows B.
54 rows A.
34 rows C.
28 rows A.
34 rows B.
54 rows A.
4 rows C.
4 rows A.
4 rows C.
4 rows A.
4 rows C.
30 rows A.
With A, bind off.

Finishing
Weave in ends.
Block to measurements. ■

Gauge
18 sts and 34 rows to 4"/10cm over garter st using size 8 (5mm) needles.
Take time to check gauge

Bull's Eye

Take a break from all the angles and give this fun circular blanket a try,
with stripes that gradually decrease to a circular center.

DESIGNED BY CLEO MALONE

Knitted Measurements
Diameter Approx 29"/73.5cm

Materials
▨ 3 3½oz/100g hanks (each approx 150yd/137.5m) of Cascade Yarns *220 Superwash Aran* (superwash merino wool) in #821 Daffodil (A) (4)
▨ 2 hanks in #871 White (B)
▨ One size 8 (5mm) circular needle, in each of the following lengths: 16, 24, 40, and 60"/40, 60, 100, and 150cm long, *or size to obtain gauge*
▨ One set (5) size 8 (5mm) double-pointed needles (dpn)
▨ Stitch marker

Note
Begin with longest circular needle and change to shorter needles, eventually to dpn, when sts no longer fit comfortably on each needle.

Blanket
With longest circular needle and A, cast on 476 sts. Join, taking care not to twist sts, and pm for beg of rnd. Purl 7 rnds.

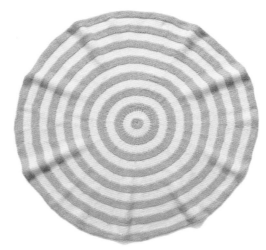

Dec rnd 1 Join B, *k12, k2tog; rep from * around—442 sts. Knit 6 rnds. Cut B.
Dec rnd 2 Join A, *k11, k2tog; rep from * around—408 sts. Purl 6 rnds. Cut A.
Dec rnd 3 Join B, *k10, k2tog; rep from * around—374 sts. Knit 6 rnds. Cut B.
Dec rnd 4 Join A, *k9, k2tog; rep from

* around—340 sts. Purl 6 rnds. Cut A.
Dec rnd 5 Join B, *k8, k2tog; rep from * around—306 sts. Knit 6 rnds. Cut B.
Dec rnd 6 Join A, *k7, k2tog; rep from * around—272 sts. Purl 6 rnds. Cut A.
Dec rnd 7 Join B, *k6, k2tog; rep from* around—238 sts. Knit 6 rnds. Cut B.
Dec rnd 8 Join A, *k5, k2tog; rep from * around—204 sts. Purl 6 rnds. Cut A.
Dec rnd 9 Join B, *k4, k2tog; rep from * around—170 sts. Knit 6 rnds. Cut B.
Dec rnd 10 Join A, *k3, k2tog; rep from * around—136 sts. Purl 6 rnds. Cut A.
Dec rnd 11 Join B, *k2, k2tog; rep from * around—102 sts. Knit 6 rnds. Cut B.
Dec rnd 12 Join A, *k1, k2tog; rep from * around—68 sts. Purl 6 rnds. Cut A.
Dec rnd 13 Join B, *k2tog; rep from * around—34 sts. Knit 6 rnds. Cut B.
Dec rnd 14 Join A, *k2tog; rep from * around—17 sts. Purl 3 rnds. Cut A. Draw tail through rem sts, pull to cinch sts, and secure.

Finishing
Weave in ends.
Block to measurements. ■

Gauge
21 sts and 28 rows to 4"/10cm over St st using size 8 (5mm) needles.
Take time to check gauge.

32

Rainbow Layer Cake

Mouthwatering shades set off by white borders
make this rainbow-striped blanket look good enough to eat!

DESIGNED BY BEA NARETTO

■□□□

Knitted Measurements
Approx 25 x 34"/63.5 x 86.5cm

Materials
■ 3 3½oz/100g balls (each approx
220yd/200m) of Cascade Yarns *220
Superwash* (superwash wool) in #871
White (A) ③
■ 2 balls in #849 Dark Aqua (B)
■ 1 ball each in #1986 Purple Hyacinth
(C), #837 Berry Pink (D), #824 Yellow (E),
and #906 Chartreuse (F)
■ One pair size 6 (4mm) needles,
or size to obtain gauge

Note
Yarn is held double throughout.

Blanket
With 2 strands of A held together, cast
on 96 sts. Work in garter st (k every row)
and stripe sequence using 2 strands as foll:
12 rows A.
*20 rows B.
4 rows A.
20 rows C.

4 rows A.
20 rows D.
4 rows A.
20 rows E.
4 rows A.
20 rows F.
4 rows A.
Rep from * once more.
20 rows B.
12 rows A.
Bind off.

SIDE BORDERS
With 2 strands of A held tog, cast on
6 sts. Work in garter st for 283 rows or
until piece is same length as blanket,
including top and bottom borders. Bind
off. With WS facing and one strand of A,
use mattress st to join side border to side
edge of blanket by weaving through the
garter bumps of each to make a flat seam.
Rep for other side.

Finishing
Weave in ends.
Block to measurements. ■

Gauge
17 sts and 33 rows to 4"/10cm over garter st, with 2 strands of yarn held tog, using size 6 (4mm) needles.
Take time to check gauge.

33

Sail Whales

A flotilla of cheeky whales sails across this fun and utterly adorable blanket;
whale bodies are knit intarsia-style, then embellished after the knitting's done.

DESIGNED BY AMY BAHRT

Knitted Measurements
Approx 28 x 33"/71 x 84cm

Materials
- 2 3½oz/100g balls (each approx 220yd/200m) of Cascade Yarns *220 Superwash* (superwash wool) in #871 White (A), #848 Blueberry (B), and #820 Lemon (C)
- 1 ball in #1952 Blaze (D)
- One size 7 (4.5mm) circular needle, 32"/80 cm long, *or size to obtain gauge*
- One pair size 7 (4.5mm) needles
- One pair size 5 (3.75mm) needles
- Stitch markers
- Three 5/16"/8mm buttons in blue

Note As small buttons are a choking hazard, embroider eyes if giving blanket to a child.
- Sewing thread to match buttons
- Sewing needle
- Embroidery needle
- Small amount of polyester stuffing

Stripe Pattern 1
Row 1 (RS) With B, knit.
Row 2 With B, purl.
Row 3 With A, knit.

Row 4 With A, purl.
Rep rows 1–4 for stripe pat 1.

Stripe Pattern 2
Row 1 (RS) With B, knit.
Row 2 With B, purl.
Row 3 With C, knit.
Row 4 With C, purl.
Rep rows 1–4 for stripe pat 2.

Notes
1) Circular needle is used to accommodate large number of sts. Do *not* join.
2) Use a separate ball for each section of color. Twist yarns on WS to prevent holes in work.
3) When changing colors for stripes and charts, carry unused yarn between rows and twist yarns on WS to prevent holes in work.
4) Edges are always worked in garter st (k every row) while body of blanket is worked in St st (k on RS, p on WS).

Blanket
With circular needle and A, cast on 138 sts. Work in garter st for 10 rows.

STRIPE SECTION 1
Next row (RS) With A, k5 (border sts); work row 1 of stripe pat 1 to last 5 sts; with A, k5 (border sts).
Next row (WS) With A, k5; work row 2 of stripe pat 1 to last 5 sts; with A, k5. Work even as established until 4-row rep has been worked 7 times, then work rows 1 and 2 once more. Cut A and B.

Gauge
19½ sts and 27 rows to 4"/10cm over St st using larger needles.
Take time to check gauge.

Sail Whales

WHALE 1
Next row (RS) With A, k5; with C, k16, pm; work row 1 of chart 1 over 32 sts, pm; with C, k80; with A, k5.
Next row (WS) With A, k5; with C, p80, sm; work row 2 of chart 1 over 32 sts, sm; with C, p16; with A, k5.
Cont through row 32 of chart 1.
Next row (RS) With A, k5; with C, k128, removing markers; with A, k5.
Work 7 rows more, keeping all C sts in St st and all A sts in garter st.

STRIPE SECTION 2
Next row (RS) With A, k5; work row 1 of stripe pat 2 to last 5 sts; with A, k5.
Next row (WS) With A, k5; work row 2 of stripe pat 2 to last 5 sts; with A, k5.
Work even as established until 4-row rep has been worked a total of 8 times. Cut C.

WHALE 2
Next row (RS) With A, k5; with B, k48, pm; work row 1 of chart 2 over 32 sts, pm; with B, k48; with A, k5.
Next row (WS) With A, k5; with B, p48, sm; work row 2 of chart 2 over 32 sts, sm; with B, p48; with A, k5.
Cont through row 32 of chart 2.
Next row (RS) With A, k5; with B, k128, removing markers; with A, k5.
Work 7 rows more, keeping all B sts in St st and all A sts in garter st.

STRIPE SECTION 3
Next row (RS) With A, k5; work row 3 of stripe pat 1 to last 5 sts, with A, k5.
Next row (WS) With A, k5; work row 4 of stripe pat 1 to last 5 sts, with A, k5.
Beg with row 1 and cont garter borders, work even until complete 4-row rep of stripe pat 1 has been worked 7 times.

WHALE 3
Note Work chart 2, substituting C for B as background color.
Next row (RS) With A, k5; with C, k80, pm; work row 1 of chart 2 over 32 sts, pm; with C, k16; with A, k5.
Next row (WS) With A, k5; with C, p16, sm; work row 2 of chart 2 over 32 sts, sm; with C, p80; with A, k5.
Cont through row 32 of chart 1.
Next row (RS) With A, k5; with C, k128, removing markers; with A, k5.
Work 7 rows more, keeping all C sts in St st and all A sts in garter st. Cut C.

With A only, work in garter st for 10 rows. Bind off all sts knitwise.

Finishing
Weave in ends. Block to measurements.

FIN 1
With larger needles and A, cast on 5 sts, leaving a long tail for sewing.
Rows 1 and 3 (WS) Purl.
Rows 2 and 4 (RS) Knit.
Inc row 5 P1, M1 p-st, p to end—6 sts.
Row 6 Knit.
Row 7 Purl.
Row 8 Ssk, k3, M1, k1.
Row 9 Purl.
Dec row 10 Ssk, k to end—5 sts.
Inc row 11 P1, M1 p-st, p to end—6 sts.
Dec row 12 Ssk, k to end—5 sts.
Row 13 P2tog, p1, pass 2nd st over first st, ssp, pass 2nd st over first st, fasten off last st.

FIN 2 (make 2)
With larger needles and A, cast on 5 sts, leaving a long tail for sewing.
Rows 1 and 3 (WS) Purl.
Rows 2 and 4 (RS) Knit.
Inc row 5 P4, M1 p-st, p1—6 sts.

Row 6 Knit.
Row 7 Purl.
Row 8 K1, M1, k3, k2tog.
Row 9 Purl.
Dec row 10 K4, k2tog—5 sts.
Inc row 11 P4, M1 p-st, p1—6 sts.
Dec row 12 K4, k2tog—5 sts.
Row 13 P2tog, p1, pass 2nd st over first st, ssp, pass 2nd st over first st, fasten off last st.

Fin Edging
With embroidery needle and A, chain st along side and top edges of each fin. Using charts as guide and long tail from cast-on, sew fin 1 to whale 1, and fin 2 to whales 2 and 3.

EYES
With embroidery needle and thread, sew one button or embroider eye to each whale as shown on charts.

MOUTH
With embroidery needle and D, chain st smile as shown on charts.

HAT
With embroidery needle and D, chain st across each hat as shown on charts.

Pompoms (make 2 with B, 1 with C)
With smaller needles cast on 7 sts. Work in St st for 7 rows, ending with a RS row. Lift first 6 sts over last st worked—1 st rem.
Cut yarn, leaving a long tail, and thread through rem st, then around other 3 edges. Place a small amount of polyester stuffing in center of pompom,
then pull up on tail to close.
Use tail to sew pompoms to top of caps as shown on charts: B pompoms to whales 1 and 3, C pompom to whale 2. ■

CHART 1

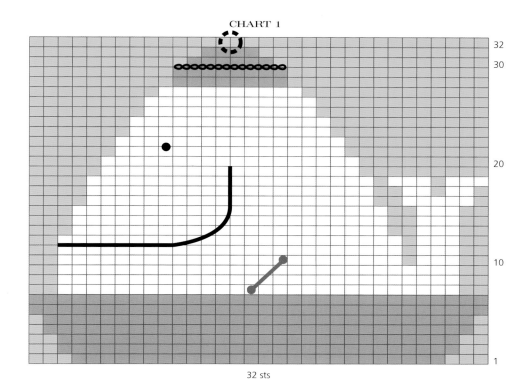

32
30

20

10

1

32 sts

COLOR KEY

▢ A

◼ B

▢ C

▨ D

PLACEMENT KEY

⭕ pompom placement

⌐ chain st mouth placement

⊙ chain st embroidery

❘ fin placement

● eye (button) placement

* Whale 3 is worked from Chart 2, using C as background color

CHART 2*

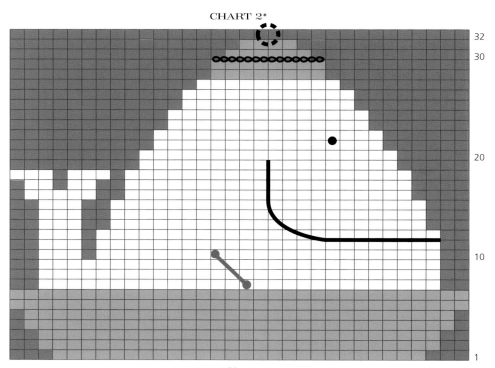

32
30

20

10

1

32 sts

101

34

Toot-Toot Truck

Got a tot who's fascinated by trucks?
Whip up this supercute blanket—and don't forget the teddy bear truck driver!

DESIGNED BY PHYLLIS ROWLEY

Knitted Measurements
Approx 26½ x 24½"/67.5 x 62cm

Materials
■ 3 3½oz/100g balls (each approx 220yd/200m) of Cascade Yarns *220 Superwash* (superwash wool) in #875 Feather Grey (A) 🎱
■ 2 balls in #808 Sunset Orange (B)
■ 1 ball each in #815 Black (C), #1926 Doeskin Heather (D), and #1944 Westpoint Blue Heather (E)
■ One pair size 6 (4mm) needles, *or size to obtain gauges*
■ Stitch markers
■ Stitch holders
■ Small amount of fiberfill

Notes
1) Blanket is knit in individual squares, picking up stitches for next square along edges of previous squares, starting at lower left corner of blanket.
2) Follow diagram for color placement and order of knitting squares.
3) Bear is worked back and forth, then sewn together at center back.

Blanket
STRIP 1
Square 1
With A, cast on 21 sts.
Row 1 (WS) K to last st, p1.
Row 2 (RS) Sl 1, k to center 3 sts, SK2P, k to last st, p1—2 sts dec'd.
Row 3 Sl 1, k to last st, p1.
Rep rows 2 and 3 eight times more—3 sts.
Next row (RS) SK2P—1 st. Do *not* fasten off; this st is first st for next square.

Square 2
With RS facing and A, pick up and k 9 sts from top of previous square, 1 st at edge (this will be center st for decreasing), and cast on 10 sts—21 sts.
Work same as square 1.

Squares 3–12
Work same as square 2. Cut yarn and pull through rem st at end of last square to fasten off.

STRIP 2
Square 1
With A, cast on 10 sts, then pick up 11 sts along right edge of square 1 of strip 1—21 sts.
Work same as square 1 of strip 1.

Square 2
With RS facing and A, pick up and k 9 sts from top of previous square, 1 st in corner where 3 squares join, then 10 sts along right edge of next square of previous strip—21 sts.
Work same as square 1 of strip 1.

Gauges
22 sts and 44 rows to 4"/10cm over garter st using size 6 (4mm) needles.
21 sts and 34 rows to 4"/10cm over St st using size 6 (4mm) needles.
Take time to check gauges.

Toot-Toot Truck

Squares 3–12
Foll colors in diagram, work same as square 2. Cut yarn and pull through rem st at end of last square to fasten off.

STRIPS 3–13
Foll colors in diagram, work same as strip 2.

DOOR
With B, work a new piece that is 2 squares high and 2 squares wide. Sew door to truck (see diagram for placement), leaving top edge open. With C, embroider door handle over 2 sts at upper right corner of door.

EDGING
With RS facing and A, pick up and k10 st along edge of one square.
Row 1 (WS) Knit.
Row 2 (RS) K to last 2 sts, k2tog—1 st dec'd.
Row 3 K2tog, k to end—1 st dec'd.
Rep rows 2 and 3 three times more, then rep row 2 again—1 st. Cut A and pull through rem st.
Rep edging along edges of rem squares.

Finishing
Weave in ends. Block to measurements.

Bear
HEAD
With D, cast on 17 sts.
Work in St st (k on RS, p on WS) for 10 rows, end with a WS row. Cut D.

YOKE
Change to E.
Row 1 (RS) Knit.
Row 2 (WS) Knit.

Rows 3 and 4 Purl.
Set-up row 5 (RS) K2, kfb, pm, kfb, k1, kfb, pm, kfb, k3, kfb, pm, kfb, k1, kfb, pm, kfb, k2—25 sts (4 sts for each back, 5 sts for each arm, and 7 sts for front).
Row 6 Purl.
Row 7 *K to 1 st before marker, kfb, sm, kfb; rep from * 3 more times, k to end—8 sts inc'd.
Rows 8 and 9 Rep rows 6 and 7—41 sts (6 sts for each back, 9 sts for each sleeve, and 11 sts for front).
Row 10 Purl.

DIVIDE ARMS AND BODY
Next row (RS) Removing markers, *k to marker, sl sleeve sts to holder; rep from * once more, k to end—23 sts.
Work even in St st for 6 rows. Cut E.

LEGS
First Leg
Change to D.
Next row (RS) K12, place rem 11 sts on holder.
Work in St st for 9 rows more.
Dec row (RS) *K2tog; rep from * to end—6 sts.
Dec row (WS) *P2tog; rep from * to end—3 sts. Cut D, leaving tail approx 10"/25.5cm for sewing. Draw tail

through rem sts and pull tight to close. Sew leg seam.

Second Leg
Return 11 held leg sts to needles. Join D.
Next row (RS) Kfb, k to end—12 sts.
Cont 2nd leg same as first leg.
After sewing leg seam, tie yarn ends tog to help hold legs tog.

ARMS
Return 9 held sleeve sts to needles. Join E.
Beg with a WS row, work in St st for 4 rows.
Next row (WS) Knit. Cut E.
Change to D.
Work in St st for 3 rows.
Dec row (RS) [K2tog] 4 times, k1—5 sts.
Dec row (WS) [P2tog] twice, p1—3 sts.
Cut D, leaving tail approx 8"/20.5cm long for sewing.
Draw tail through rem sts and pull tight to close. Sew arm seam.
Rep for 2nd arm.

Finishing
With E, sew back seam from legs to top of yoke, lightly stuffing legs and body as you sew. Do *not* stuff arms.
With C, embroider eyes, mouth, and nose using photo as guide.
With D, sew back seam to top of head. Lightly stuff head. Sew top of head closed. Sew diagonally across top and side of head for ears, about 2 sts in from edge and 2 rows down from top. ■

COLOR KEY

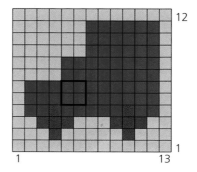

▨	A
▪	B
▪	C
☐	Door Placement

35

Crested Waves

A garter stitch background creates the perfect backdrop
for waving bands of cables on this beautiful blanket.

DESIGNED BY ANASTASIA BLAES

Knitted Measurements
Approx 28½ x 40"/72.5 x 101.5cm

Materials
- 7 3½oz/100g hanks (each approx 128yd/117m) of Cascade Yarns *128 Superwash* (superwash merino wool) in #1946 Silver (5)
- One size 10 (6mm) circular needle, 32"/80cm long, *or size to obtain gauge*
- Cable needle (cn)
- Stitch markers

Stitch Glossary
LT (left twist) Knit 2nd st on LH needle behind first st, do *not* drop from needle, knit first st and let both drop from needle.
RT (right twist) Knit 2nd st on LH needle in front of first st, do *not* drop from needle, knit first st and let both drop from needle

Notes
1) Circular needle is used to accommodate large number of sts. Do *not* join.

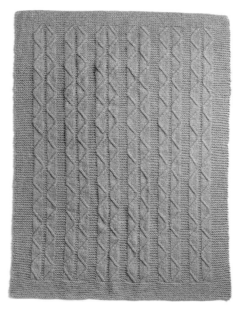

2) Cable and wave pattern can be worked from either written instructions or chart.

Cable and Wave Pattern
(over a multiple of 17 sts plus 12)
Row 1 (RS) *K3, RT, k2, LT, k8; rep from * to last 12 sts, k3, RT, k2, LT, k3.
Row 2 and all WS rows P5, k2, p5, *k5, p5, k2, p5; rep from * to end.
Row 3 *K2, RT, k4, LT, k7; rep from * to last 12 sts, k2, RT, k4, LT, k2.
Row 5 *K1, RT, k6, LT, k6; rep from * to last 12 sts, k1, RT, k6, LT, k1.
Row 7 *RT, k8, LT, k5; rep from * to last 12 sts, RT, k8, LT.
Rows 9 and 11 Knit.
Row 13 *LT, k8, RT, k5; rep from * to last 12 sts, LT, k8, RT.
Row 15 *K1, LT, k6, RT, k6; rep from * to last 12 sts, k1, LT, k6, RT, k1.
Row 17 *K2, LT, k4, RT, k7; rep from * to last 12 sts, k2, LT, k4, RT, k2.
Row 19 *K3, LT, k2, RT, k8; rep from * to last 12 sts, k3, LT, k2, RT, k3.
Rows 21 and 23 Knit.
Row 24 P5, k2, p5, *k5, p5, k2, p5; rep from * to end.
Rep rows 1–24 for cable and wave pat.

Gauge
17 sts and 24 rows to 4"/10cm in cable and wave pat using size 10 (6mm) needle.
Take time to check gauge.

Crested Waves

Blanket
Cast on 117 sts. Knit 18 rows.

BEGIN PATTERN
Set-up row (WS) K10, pm, *p5, k2, p5, k5; rep from * to last 22 sts, p5, k2, p5, pm, k10.
Row 1 (RS) K10, sm, work row 1 of cable and wave pat to last 10 sts, sm, k10. Keeping 10 sts each side in garter st (k every row), cont to foll chart in this manner to row 24, then rep rows 1–24 until piece measures approx 37¾"/96cm from beg, end with row 20 of pat. Knit 18 rows, removing markers on first row. Bind off all sts loosely knitwise.

Finishing
Weave in ends.
Block to measurements. ∎

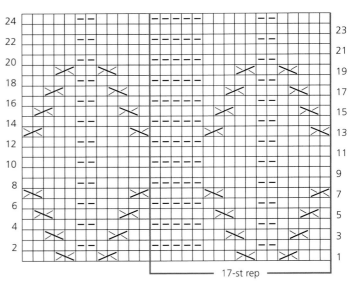

17-st rep

STITCH KEY

☐ k on RS, p on WS

⊟ p on RS, k on WS

▤ RT

▤ LT

36

Diamond in a Square

A traditional quilt pattern inspired this geometric beauty.
Modular squares and pick-up-as-you-go knitting speed the project along.

DESIGNED BY GINGER LUTERS

Knitted Measurements
Approx 35 x 35"/89 x 89cm

Materials
■ 3 3½oz/100g balls (each approx 220yd/200m) of Cascade Yarns *220 Superwash* (superwash wool) in #1960 Pacific (A) (3)
■ 2 balls each in #1997 Spring Bud (B) and #1942 Mint (C)
■ One pair size 8 (5mm) needles
or size to obtain gauge
■ Removable stitch markers
■ Stitch holders

Garter Ridge Stitch
Row 1 (WS) Knit.
Row 2 Knit.
Row 3 Purl.
Row 4 Knit.
Rep rows 1–4 for garter ridge st.

Note
1) All stitches are picked up from the RS.
2) Four mitered squares form center diamond. Solid-color triangles, knit along edges of diamond, form larger square. Bands are knit along edges of square with miters to fill each corner.

3) When changing colors, twist yarns on WS to prevent holes in work.

Blanket
STRIPED CENTER DIAMOND
With A, cast on 91 sts.

Square 1
Next row (WS) K1 tbl, k44, p1 (center st), k44, sl 1 wyif.
Cut A, then cut an extra 5½yd/5m length of A. Set this strand aside.

Begin working in garter ridge st as foll:
Row 1 (RS) With B, k1 tbl, k to 1 st before center st; with strand of A, S2KP; bring B under A; with B, k to last st, sl 1 wyif—2 sts dec'd.
Row 2 With B, k1 tbl, k to 1 st before center st; bring A forward and p2; with B, k to last st, sl 1 wyif. Do *not* cut B; carry unused yarn along side of work.
Row 3 With C, k1 tbl, k to 1 st before center st; with A, S2KP; bring C under A; with C, k to last st, sl 1 wyif—2 sts dec'd.
Row 4 With C, k1 tbl, p to center st; bring A forward and p2; with C, p to last st, sl 1 wyif.
Cont in color sequence as established, rep rows 1–4 until 5 sts rem, end with WS row.
Next row (RS) With C, k1 tbl; with A, S2KP; with C, sl 1 wyif—3 sts.
Next row With C, k1 tbl; bring A forward and p2.
Next row With A, S2KP—1 st.
Cut all yarns and pull A through rem st.

Square 2
With A, cast on 46 sts, then with RS of square 1 facing, pick up and k 45 sts along right cast-on edge—91 sts.
Work same as square 1.

Gauge
16½ sts and 32 rows to 4"/10cm over garter ridge st using size 8 (5mm) needles.
Take time to check gauge.

Diamond in a Square

36

Square 3
With A, cast on 46 sts, then with RS of square 2 facing, pick up and k 45 sts along cast-on edge—91 sts.
Work same as square 1.

Square 4
With RS facing and A, pick up and k 45 sts along rem cast-on edge of square 1, 1 st in corner st of square 2, then 45 sts along cast-on edge of square 3—91 sts.
Work same as square 1.

CORNER TRIANGLES
Triangle 1
With A and RS facing, pick up and k 90 sts along edges of squares 1 and 2 (see diagram). Work in garter ridge st as foll:
Row 1 (WS) Knit.
Row 2 K1, ssk, k to last 3 sts, k2tog, k1—2 sts dec'd.
Row 3 Purl.
Row 4 Rep row 2—2 sts dec'd.
Row 5 Knit.
Rep rows 2–5 until 6 sts rem, end with a WS row.
Next row Ssk, k2, k2tog—4 sts.
Next row Purl.
Next row Ssk, k2tog—2 sts.
Next row Purl.
Next row K2tog—1 st.
Cut yarn and pull through rem st.

Triangles 2, 3, and 4
Work same as triangle 1 along edges of squares 2 and 3, squares 3 and 4, and then squares 4 and 1.

BORDERS
With C and RS facing, pick up and k 128 sts along edges of triangles 1 and 2.

Row 1 (WS) K1 tbl, k to last st, sl 1 wyif.
Rep row 1 twice more.
With B, rep row 1 eight times more.
With A, rep row 1 twice more.

Picot bind-off
Next row (RS) Bind off 2 sts, *sl st on RH needle back to LH needle; using knitted cast-on method, cast on 1 st; bind off 4 sts; rep from * until 1 st rem. Place last st on holder and cut A, leaving a 30"/76cm tail for picot edge along mitered corners.

Rep side border 1 and picot bind-off along rem 3 edges of blanket; do *not* pick up sts along borders.

CORNERS
With A and RS facing, beg at any bound-off edge of border, pick up and k 7 sts along one side border edge, 1 st in point of triangle, then 7 sts along adjoining side border edge—15 sts.
Row 1 (WS) K1 tbl, k to center st, p1, k to last st, sl 1 wyif.
Row 2 K1 tbl, k to 1 st before center st,

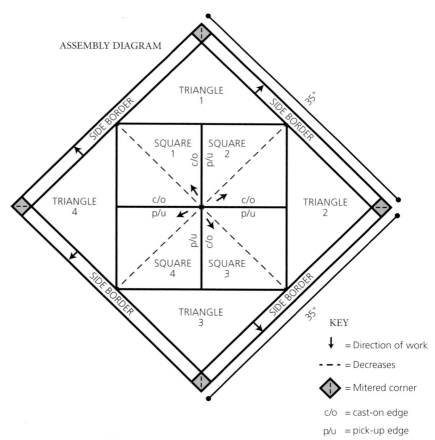

ASSEMBLY DIAGRAM

TRIANGLE 1

SIDE BORDER

SIDE BORDER

35"

SQUARE 1

SQUARE 2

c/o

p/u

TRIANGLE 4

c/o

c/o

TRIANGLE 2

p/u

p/u

SQUARE 4

p/u

c/o

SQUARE 3

SIDE BORDER

TRIANGLE 3

SIDE BORDER

35"

KEY

↓ = Direction of work

- - - = Decreases

◈ = Mitered corner

c/o = cast-on edge

p/u = pick-up edge

S2KP, k to last st, sl 1 wyif—2 sts dec'd.
Rep rows 1 and 2 until 5 sts rem, end
with a WS row.
Next row (RS) K1 tbl, S2KP, sl 1 wyif—3 sts.
Next row K1 tbl, p1, sl 1 wyif.
Next row S2KP—1 st.
Cut yarn and pull through last st.
Mark as center st.
Rep for rem 3 corners.

Picot edge
Begin at right edge of any corner with
RS facing, put held st from picot bind-off
onto RH needle; with 30"/76cm tail, pick
up and k 1 st in first st of pick-up row,
bind off 1 st, *pick up and k 1 st in first
st of next RS row, bind off 1 st, sl rem st
back to LH needle, using knitted cast-on
method, cast on 1 st, [pick up and k 1 st
in first st of next RS row, bind off 1 st]
twice; rep from * 4 times more, working
a cast-on st at marked st—5 picots.
Remove marker.
Rep on 3 rem corners.

Finishing
Weave in ends, using tail of A to close
any rem holes in blanket center.
Block to measurements. ■

Swimming Upstream

An easy slip-stitch pattern gives this toasty salmon-colored blanket
the cozy speckled look.

DESIGNED BY MARI TOBITA

Knitted Measurements
Approx 28 x 39"/71 x 99cm

Materials
- 3   3½oz/100g balls (each approx 220yd/200m) of Cascade Yarns *220 Superwash* (superwash wool) in #827 Coral (A)
- 2 balls each #910A Winter White (B) and #1941 Salmon (C)
- One size 6 (4mm) circular needle, 32"/80cm long, *or size to obtain gauges*
- One size 6 (4mm) circular needle, 60"/152cm long
- One size G/6 (4mm) crochet hook
- Stitch markers
- Contrasting scrap yarn

Notes
1) Carry yarns currently not in use along side of blanket.
2) All stitches are slipped purlwise with yarn in back.
3) Check pattern can be worked from chart or written instructions.

Check Pattern
(over a multiple of 4 sts plus 4)
Row 1 (WS) With A, purl.

Row 2 (RS) With B, k1, sl 2 wyib, *k2, sl 2 wyib; rep from * to last st, k1.
Row 3 With B, p1, *sl 2 wyif, p2; rep from * to last 3 sts, sl 2 wyif, p1.
Row 4 With A, knit.
Row 5 With C, p1, *p2, sl 2 wyif; rep from * to last 3 sts, p3.

Row 6 With C, k3, *sl 2 wyib, k2; rep from * to last st, k1.
Rep rows 1–6 for check pat.

Blanket
NOTE Circular needle is used to accommodate large number of stitches. Do *not* join.
With A, cast on 180 sts using provisional cast-on (see page 182). With shorter needle, work rows 1–6 of check pat until piece measures approx 38"/96.5cm, end with row 3.

GARTER EDGING
With longer needle, A, and RS facing, k across row, pm, and pick up and k 202 sts evenly along left edge of blanket.
Cut A, pm, remove scrap yarn from provisional cast-on, sl these sts to needle, and pm. Rejoin A and pick up and k 202 sts evenly along right edge of blanket, pm for beg of rnd, and join to work in the rnd—764 sts.
Dec rnd 1 With A, [p2, *p2tog, p4; rep from * to 4 sts before marker, p2tog, p2, sm, p to next marker, sm] twice—60 sts dec'd.
Cut A.

Gauges
26 sts and 45 rows to 4"/10cm over check pat using size 6 (4mm) needle.
21 sts and 48 rows to 4"/10cm over garter st using size 6 (4mm) needle.
Take time to check gauges.

Swimming Upstream

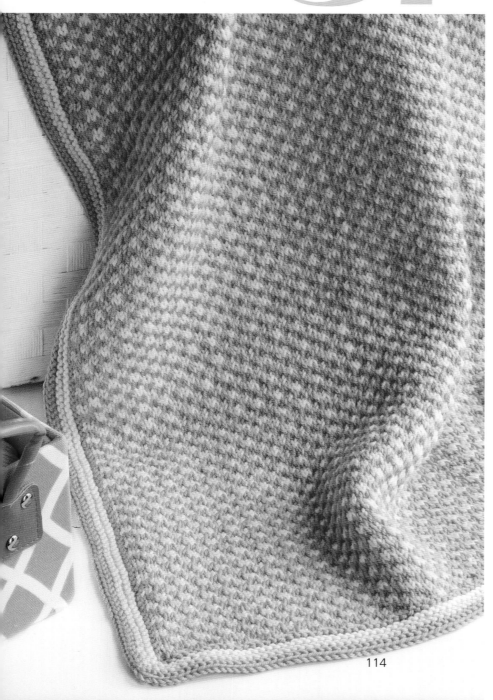

Inc rnd 2 With B, [kfb, k to 1 st before marker, kfb, sm] 4 times—8 sts inc'd.
Rnd 3 Purl.
Cut B.
Rnds 4 and 5 With C, rep rnds 2 and 3—8 sts inc'd.
Cut C.
Inc rnd 6 With A, rep rnds 2 and 3—8 sts inc'd.
Rnd 7 Purl.
Rnd 8 [Kfb, bind off all sts to 1 st before marker, kfb, bind off these sts and remove marker] 4 times.

Finishing
Weave in ends.
Block to measurements. ■

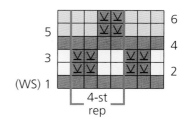

STITCH KEY

☐ k on RS, p on WS

Ⅴ slip 1 wyib on RS,
slip 1 wyif on WS

COLOR KEY

▨ A

☐ B

☐ C

38

Diamond Twist

Crisp cables and fresh stripes give this blanket a nautical look.
Pick a solid color, like this cool sea-blue, so that the lovely diamond pattern pops.

DESIGNED BY BEA NARETTO

Knitted Measurements
Approx 27 x 37½"/68.5 x 95cm

Materials
- 9 3½oz/100g hanks (each approx 128yd/117m) of Cascade Yarns *128 Superwash* (superwash merino wool) in #231 Blue Mist (A) (5)
- 1 hank in #871 White (B)
- One pair size 11 (8mm) needles, *or size to obtain gauge*
- Stitch markers
- Cable needle (cn)

Stitch Glossary
2-st LC Sl 1 st to cn and hold to *front*, k1, k1 from cn.
2-st RPC Sl 1 st to cn and hold to *back*, k1, p1 from cn.
2-st LPC Sl 1 st to cn and hold to *front*, p1, k1 from cn.

Ribbed Border
(over a multiple of 4 sts plus 4)
Row 1 (RS) Sl 1 knitwise, *p2, k2; rep from * to last 3 sts, p2, p1 tbl.
Row 2 Sl 1 knitwise, *k2, p2; rep from * to last 3 sts, k2, p1 tbl.
Rep rows 1 and 2 for ribbed border.

Diamond Twist Stitch
(over a multiple of 8 sts plus 10)
Row 1 P1, *p3, 2-st LC, p3; rep from * to last 9 sts, p3, 2-st LC, p4.
Row 2 K3, 2-st LPC, 2-st RPC, k2, *k2, 2-st LPC, 2-st RPC, k2; rep from * to last st, k1.

Row 3 P1, *p1, 2-st RPC, p2, 2-st LPC, p1; rep from * to last 9 sts, p1, 2-st RPC, p2, 2-st LPC, p2.
Row 4 K1, 2-st LPC, k4, 2-st RPC, *2-st LPC, k4, 2-st RPC; rep from * to last st, k1.
Row 5 P1, k1, *p6, 2-st LC; rep from * to last 8 sts, p6, k1, p1.
Row 6 K1, 2-st RPC, k4, 2-st LPC, *2-st RPC, k4, 2-st LPC; rep from * to last st, k1.
Row 7 P1, *p1, 2-st LPC, p2, 2-st RPC, p1; rep from * to last 9 sts, p1, 2-st LPC, p2, 2-st RPC, p2.
Row 8 K3, 2-st RPC, 2-st LPC, k2, *k2, 2-st RPC, 2-st LPC, k2; rep from * to last st, k1.
Rep rows 1–8 for diamond twist st.

Notes
1) Yarn is held double throughout.
2) For ribbed top and bottom borders, carry yarns not in use along side of blanket.
3) 2-st RPC and 2-st LPC are worked on both RS and WS of blanket.
3) Diamond twist stitch can be worked from written instructions or chart.

Blanket
BOTTOM BORDER
With 2 strands of A, cast on 92 sts.
Work ribbed border for 8 rows.

Gauge
13½ sts and 16 rows to 4"/10cm over diamond twist st, with 2 strands of yarn held tog, using size 11 (8mm) needles.
Take time to check gauge.

38
Diamond Twist

With 2 strands of B, work rib for 2 rows.
With A, work rib for 2 rows.
Rep last 4 rows once more.
Cut B.

BEGIN DIAMOND TWIST STITCH
Next row (RS) Work first 13 sts as
established, pm, work row 1 of diamond
twist st over 66 sts, pm, work rem 13 sts
as established.
Cont in diamond twist st, keeping first
and last 13 sts in ribbed border, until
piece measures approx 33½"/85cm, end
with a row 8.
Remove markers.

TOP BORDER
With A, work in ribbed border for 2 rows.
With 2 strands of B, work rib for 2 rows.
Rep last 4 rows once more.
Cut B.
With A, work in established rib for 8 rows.
Bind off all sts in pat.

Finishing
Weave in ends.
Block to measurements. ■

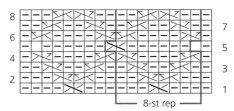

8-st rep

STITCH KEY

☐ k on RS

— p on RS, k on WS

⧓ 2-st LC

⧄ 2-st RPC

⧅ 2-st LPC

39

Simply Stripes

A trio of cool colors form symmetric stripes against a neutral gray background.
Change up the contrast colors to match your little one's nursery!

DESIGNED BY ANN FAITH

Knitted Measurements
Approx 25 x 35"/63.5 x 89cm

Materials
■ 5 3½oz/100g hanks (each approx 150yd/137.5m) of Cascade Yarns *220 Superwash Aran* (superwash merino wool) in #1946 Silver Grey (A) ④
■ 1 hank each in #845 Denim (B), #849 Dark Aqua (C), and #240 Jasmine Green (D)
■ One size 8 (5mm) circular needle, 24"/60cm long, *or size to obtain gauge*

Notes
1) Circular needle is used to accommodate large number of sts. Do *not* join.
2) Cut yarns for each color change. Do not carry unused colors along side of blanket.

Blanket
With A, cast on 108 sts. Work in garter st (k every row) for 3"/7.5cm, end with a WS row.
With B, knit 16 rows.
With A, knit 12 rows.
With C, knit 16 rows.
With A, knit 12 rows.
With D, knit 16 rows.
With A, work in garter st until piece measures 24"/61cm from beg, end with a WS row.
With D, knit 16 rows.
With A, knit 12 rows.
With C, knit 16 rows.
With A, knit 12 rows.
With B, knit 16 rows.
With A, work in garter st for 3"/7.5cm, end with a WS row. Bind off.

Finishing
Weave in ends.
Block to measurements. ■

Gauge
18 sts and 36 rows to 4"/10cm over garter st using size 8 (5mm) needles.
Take time to check gauge.

40 Tricolor Stars

Everyone who sees this beautiful blanket,
knit with three colors in a cluster star stitch, will be star-struck!

DESIGNED BY LINDA MEDINA

Knitted Measurements
Approx 23 x 34"/58.5 x 86.5cm

Materials
■ 2 3½oz/100g balls (each approx
220yd/200m) of Cascade Yarns *220
Superwash* (superwash wool) each in
#874 Ridge Rock (A) and #817 Aran (B) (3)
■ 1 ball in #229 Ash Rose (C)
■ Size 7 (4.5mm) circular needle,
40"/100cm long, *or size to obtain gauge*

Note
Circular needle is used to accommodate
large number of sts. Do *not* join.

Closed Star Stitch
(over a multiple of 3 sts plus 2)
Row 1 (RS) With A, k1, *k3, pass the
first of 3 knit sts over 2nd and 3rd sts
and off RH needle; rep from * to last st, k1.
Row 2 (WS) With B, p1, *insert RH
needle from WS under passed st from
previous row and purl in this st, p2; rep
from * to last st, p1.
Row 3 With B, p2, *k3, pass first of 3
knit sts over 2nd and 3rd sts and off RH
needle; rep from * to end.

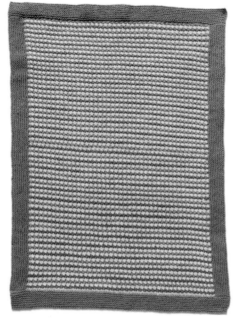

Row 4 With C, *insert RH needle from WS
under passed st from previous row and purl
in this st, p2; rep from * to last 2 sts, p2.
Row 5 With C, rep row 1.

Row 6 With B, rep row 2.
Row 7 With B, rep row 3.
Row 8 With A, rep row 4.
Rep rows 1–8 for closed star st.

Blanket
With A, cast on 131 sts.

BEGIN CLOSED STAR STITCH PATTERN
Set-up row (WS) With A, purl.
Work rows 1–8 of closed star st pat 26
times, then work rows 1–7 once more.
With B, bind off.
Block lightly before working borders.

SIDE BORDERS
With RS facing and A, pick up and k 160
sts evenly along side edge. Knit 16 rows.
Bind off.
Rep for rem side edge.

TOP AND BOTTOM BORDERS
With RS facing and A, pick up and k 120
sts evenly along bottom edge.
Knit 16 rows. Bind off.
Rep for top edge.

Finishing
Weave in ends. ■

Gauge
27 sts and 29 rows to 4"/10cm over closed star st, after blocking, using size 7 (4.5mm) needles.
Take time to check gauge.

Eyelet Rhombus

Eyelets line up to form the rhombus-shaped motifs stacked in rows on this blanket.
Make your blanket larger by adding repeats to length or width.

DESIGNED BY JESIE OSTERMILLER

Knitted Measurements
Approx 31 x 19"/78.5 x 48.5cm

Materials
- 3 3½oz/100g skeins (each approx 220yd/200m) of Cascade Yarns *220 Superwash Merino* (superwash merino wool) in #18 Violet Tulip ⓶
- One size 7 (4.5mm) circular needle, 24"/60cm long, *or size to obtain gauges*
- Stitch markers

Notes
1) Circular needle is used to accommodate large number of sts. Do *not* join.
2) Blanket size can be easily increased by adding more repeats in width or length. Adjust yarn amounts accordingly.

Blanket
Cast on 128 sts. Work in garter st (k every row) for 2"/5cm.

BEGIN CHART PATTERN
Next (RS) K12, pm, work the 13-st rep of chart 8 times, pm, k12.
Keeping 104 sts between markers in

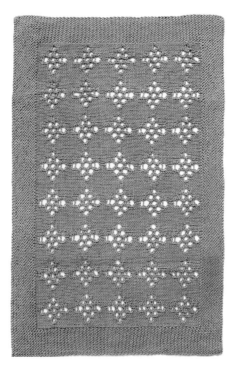

chart pat and rem sts in garter st, work chart through row 18, then rep rows 1–18 four times more.

TOP BORDER
Next row (RS) Knit, removing markers. Cont in garter st until top border measures 2"/5cm, end with a RS row. Bind off all sts knitwise.

Finishing
Weave in ends.
Block to measurements. ■

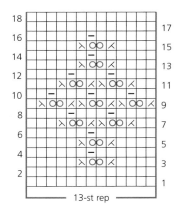

13-st rep

STITCH KEY
☐ k on RS, p on WS
⊟ p on RS, k on WS
⊠ k2tog
⊠ ssk
⊡⊡ yo twice

Gauges
16 sts and 24 rows to 4"/10cm over eyelet pat using size 7 (4.5mm) needle.
One chart repeat measures approx 3¼"/8.5cm wide and 3"/7.5cm tall.
Take time to check gauges.

Triple Ripple

A classic chevron pattern looks fresh and fantastic in cheery brights, adding a burst of color to crib or stroller.

DESIGNED BY MARGRET WILLSON

Knitted Measurements
Approx 26 x 35½"/66 x 90cm

Materials
- 3 3½oz/100g hanks (each approx 128yd/117m) of Cascade Yarns *128 Superwash* (superwash merino wool) in #1946 Silver (A) (5)
- 2 hanks each in #820 Lemon (B) and #218 Opal (C)
- One size 10 (6mm) circular needle, 24"/40cm long, *or size to obtain gauge*

Note
Circular needle is used to accommodate large number of stitches. Do *not* join.

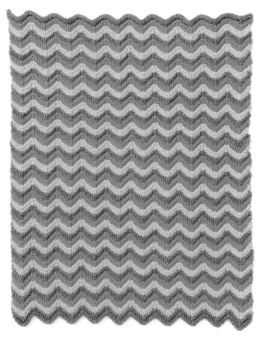

Chevron Stitch Pattern
(over a multiple of 13 sts)
Rows 1 and 3 (RS) *Kfb, k4, SK2P, k4, kfb; rep from * to end.
Row 2 Purl.
Row 4 Knit.
Rep rows 1–4 for chevron st pat.

Blanket
With A, cast on 130 sts.
Knit 1 row.
*Working in chevron st pat, work 4 rows A, 4 rows B, 4 rows C; rep from * 14 times more, then work 4 rows A. With A, bind off.

Finishing
Weave in ends.
Block to measurements. ■

Gauge
20 sts and 20 rows to 4"/10cm over chevron st pat using size 10 (6mm) needle.
Take time to check gauge.

43

Kilim Mosaic

This sensational blanket is knit in a mosaic-stitch motif inspired by Asian tapestry, then finished with fun faux fur stitch.

DESIGNED BY KATHARINE HUNT

Knitted Measurements
Approx 23 x 36½"/58.5 x 92.5cm

Materials
- 4 3½oz/100g balls (each approx 220yd/200m) of Cascade Yarns *220 Superwash* (superwash wool) in #1973 Seafoam Heather (A) (3)
- 3 balls in #842 Light Iris (B)
- One pair size 7 (4.5mm) needles, *or size to obtain gauge*
- One pair size 8 (5mm) needles
- One size 7 (4.5mm) circular needle, 32"/80cm long
- Scrap yarn
- One size H/8 (5mm) crochet hook

Stitch Glossary
LS (loop stitch) Knit next st but leave it on LH needle; bring yarn to front between needles and wind it around left thumb; bring yarn to back and k into the same st on LH needle; sl st off LH needle; sl 2 sts from RH needle back to LH needle; k2tog tbl, then tug on loop to secure.

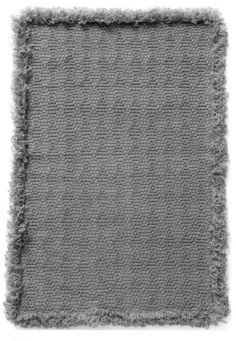

Notes
1) Chart shows only one row for both RS and WS rows. Read RS rows from right to left, and WS rows from left to right. Knit each row with color shown on first and last stitches (also noted next to row number for RS row), slipping stitches of opposite color with yarn held at WS of work.
2) Chart is worked in garter st (k every row).

Blanket
With A, smaller needles, and using provisional cast-on, cast on 113 sts (see page 182).
Knit 1 row.

BEGIN CHART
Join B and work chart, working 10-st rep 10 times each row.
Cont in established pat until piece measures approx 34½"/78.5cm from beg, end with row 2 of chart. Cut B.
Place sts on circular needle.

Finishing
Block to measurements.

TOP BORDER
With circular needle and A, with WS facing, work top border as foll:
Inc row 1 (WS) M1, k to last st, M1— 2 sts inc'd.

Gauge
21½ sts and 43 rows to 4"/10cm over chart pat using smaller needles.
Take time to check gauge.

Kilim Mosaic

Row 2 (RS) K1, work LS in every st to last st, k1.
Rep rows 1 and 2 twice more—119 sts.
With larger needle, bind off all sts knitwise.

BOTTOM BORDER
With WS facing, circular needle, and A, remove
scrap yarn from provisional cast-on and place 113
sts on smaller needle.
Work same as for top border.

SIDE BORDERS
With RS facing, circular needle, and A, pick up and
k 168 sts evenly along one side edge.
Work side border same as top border—174 sts.
Rep for rem side border.
Sew borders tog along mitered corners.
Weave in ends. Do *not* block borders. ■

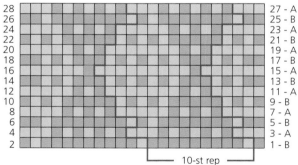

COLOR KEY

□ A

■ B

Whale Watching

You'll have a whale of a time knitting this adorable blanket,
with rows of orcas swimming across the sea.

DESIGNED BY KATARINA SEGERBRAND

Knitted Measurements
Approx 25 x 34¾"/63.5 x 88.5 cm

Materials
- 2 3½oz/100g balls (each approx 220yd/200m) of Cascade Yarns *220 Superwash* (superwash wool) in #856 Aporto (A) **3**
- 3 balls in #817 Aran (B)
- 1 ball in #252 Celestial (C)
- One size 6 (4mm) circular needle, 24"/60 cm long, *or size to obtain gauge*
- Stitch markers

Seed Stitch
(over an odd number of sts)
Row 1 *K1, p1; rep from * to last st, k1.
Row 2 P the knit sts and k the purl sts.
Rep row 2 for seed st.

Notes
1) Use a separate ball of yarn for each seed stitch border when working the charted portion of the blanket.
2) Chart is worked in St st (k on RS, p on WS).
3) When changing colors, twist yarns on WS to prevent holes in work.
4) When working whales, drop C at end of last whale, and twist colors when picking up C on next row.
5) Circular needle is used to accommodate large number of sts. Do *not* join.

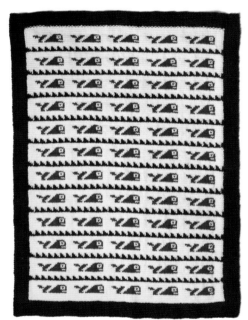

Blanket
BOTTOM BORDER
With A, cast on 145 sts.
Work in seed st for 1¾"/4.5 cm.

BEGIN CHART
Next row (RS) With A, work 10 sts as established, pm; work first 5 sts and then 24-st rep of chart row 1 five times, pm; with new ball of A, work to end as established.
Next row (WS) With A, work to marker as established, sm; work 24-st rep five times and then last 5 sts of chart row 2, sm; with A, work to end as established.
Cont foll chart in this manner through row 19; rep rows 20–38 ten times; then work rows 39–61 once.
Piece should measure approx 33"/84cm from beg. Cut B.

TOP BORDER
With A, work in seed st over all sts for 1¾"/4.5cm, removing markers on first row.
Bind off all sts in pat.

Finishing
Weave in ends.
Block to measurements. ∎

Gauge
23 sts and 29 rows to 4"/10cm over St st and chart using size 6 (4mm) needles.
Take time to check gauge.

Whale Watching

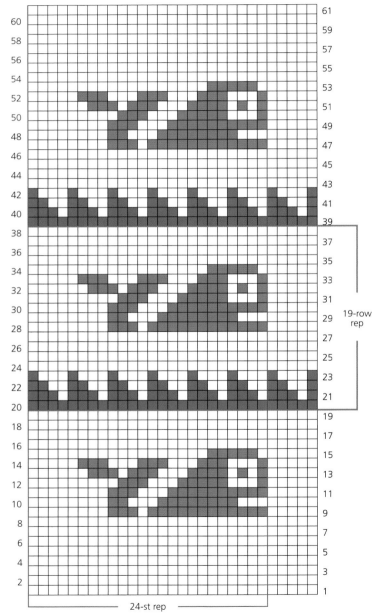

COLOR KEY

- ■ A
- □ B
- ■ C

24-st rep

19-row rep

Graceful Gradients

A delightful chevron pattern and gradually morphing colors
make this blanket fun to knit and a treat for a special baby.

DESIGNED BY CHERYL MURRAY

Knitted Measurements
Approx 23½ x 34"/59.5 x 86.5cm

Materials
▓ 1 3½oz/100g ball (each approx
220yd/200m) of Cascade Yarns *220
Superwash* (superwash wool) each in
#837 Berry Pink (A), #901 Cotton Candy
(B), #836 Pink Ice (C), #894 Strawberry
Cream (D), and #871 White (E) ⬤
▓ One size 8 (5mm) circular needle,
32"/80cm long, *or size to obtain gauge*

Note
Circular needle is used to accommodate
large number of sts. Do *not* join.

Blanket
With A, cast on 114 sts.
Work in garter st (k every row) for 6 rows.

STRIPE 1
Beg with a RS row, work chart 1 as foll:
Row 1 (RS) K5 (5-st border), work 16-st

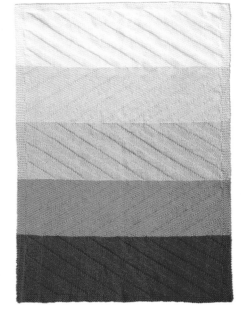

rep 6 times, work next 8 sts after rep, k5
(5-st border).
Cont chart as established through row 48.

STRIPE 2
Next row (RS) With B, knit.
Beg with a WS row, work chart 2 as foll:
Row 1 (WS) K5 (5-st border), work next
8 sts before rep, work 16-st rep 6 times,
k5 (5-st border).
Cont chart as established through row 47.

STRIPE 3
Next row (RS) With C, knit.
Beg with a WS row, work chart 3 as foll:
Row 1 (WS) K5 (5-st border), work next
8 sts before rep, work 16-st rep 6 times,
k5 (5-st border).
Cont in chart as established through row 47.

STRIPE 4
Next row (RS) With D, knit.
Beg with a WS row, work rows 1–47 of
chart 2 as before.

Gauge
19 sts and 30 rows to 4"/10cm over chevron pat using size 8 (5mm) needle.
Take time to check gauge.

Graceful Gradients

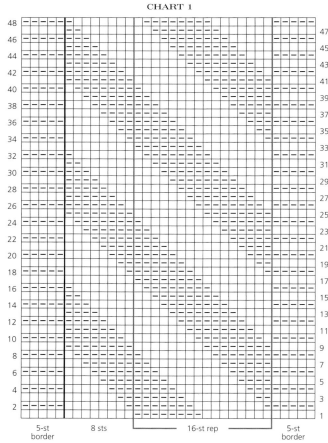

CHART 1

STRIPE 5
Next row (RS) With E, knit.
Beg with a WS row, work rows 1–47 of chart 3 as before.
Next row (RS) Work row 1 of chart 1 as before.
Work in garter st for 6 rows.
Bind off knitwise on WS.

Finishing
Weave in ends.
Block to measurements. ■

CHART 2

CHART 3

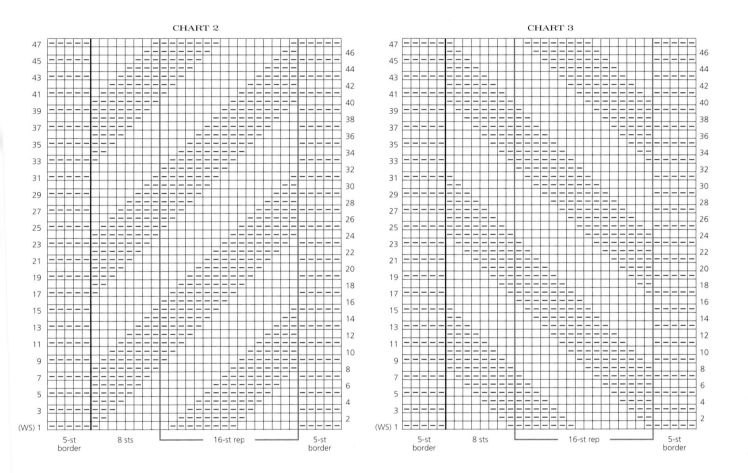

STITCH KEY

☐ k on RS, p on WS

⊟ p on RS, k on WS

135

Oxford Stripes

Turn the boring blue Oxford stripe on its head by replacing
with vivid coral and silver—or pick another pair of mod colors.

DESIGNED BY YOKO HATTA

Knitted Measurements
Approx 21 x 24½"/53.5 x 62cm

Materials
■ 2 3½oz/100g hanks (each approx
150yd/137.5m) of Cascade Yarns *220
Superwash Aran* (superwash merino
wool) each in #1946 Silver Grey (A)
and #242 Deep Sea Coral (B) (4)
■ One size 8 (5mm) circular needle,
40"/100cm long, *or size to obtain gauge*

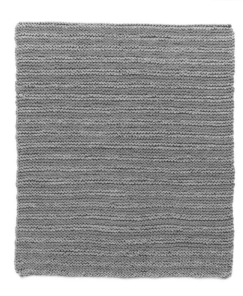

Notes
1) Circular needle is used to
accommodate large number of stitches.
Do *not* join.
2) Carry yarn not in use along side of row.

Blanket
With A, cast on 74 sts.
[With A, knit 4 rows; with B, knit 4 rows]
21 times.
With A, knit 3 rows.
With A, bind off.

Finishing
Weave in ends.
Block to measurements. ■

Gauge
14 sts and 28 rows to 4"/10cm over garter st using size 8 (5mm) needle.
Take time to check gauge.

Yahoo Kangaroo

Your little mate will say "G-day!" to this super-cute kangaroo
—complete with working pouch for tiny treasures.

DESIGNED BY WEI WILKINS

Knitted Measurements
Approx 41¾ x 28¾"/106 x 73cm

Materials
■ 5 3½oz/100g balls (each approx 220yd/200m) of Cascade Yarns *220 Superwash* (superwash wool) in #874 Ridge Rock (A) (3)
■ 3 balls in #877 Golden (B)
■ 1 ball in #872 Bitter Chocolate (C)
■ One each sizes 5 and 6 (3.75 and 4mm) circular needles, 32"/80cm long, *or size to obtain gauges*
■ Stitch markers

Notes
1) Circular needle is used to accommodate large number of sts. Do *not* join.
2) Use separate ball of yarn for each color section. Do *not* carry yarn across back of work. When changing colors, twist yarns on WS to prevent holes in work.
3) When embroidering kangaroo, keep yarn at same side, left or right, of needle for each stitch, especially for curves, to maintain smooth line.

4) Kangaroo charts are worked over Stockinette stitch (k on RS, p on WS).

Blanket
BOTTOM BORDER
With smaller needle and A, cast on 212 sts using a stretchy cast-on. Knit 8 rows. Change to larger needle. Knit 1 row.
Next row (WS) K5, p to last 5 sts, k5.

BEGIN BABY PINE TREE CHART
Row 1 (RS) K7, pm, work row 1 of baby pine tree chart to last 7 sts, pm, k7.
Row 2 (WS) K5, p2, sm, work row 2 of chart to marker, sm, p2, k5.

Cont to foll chart in this manner through row 20.
Next row (RS) K7, sm, work row 1 of chart over next 54 sts, k5, pm, k80, pm, k5, work row 1 of chart over next 54 sts, sm, k7.
Next row (WS) K5, p2, sm, work row 2 of chart over next 54 sts, p5, sm, p to marker, sm, p5, work next row of chart over next 54 sts, sm, p2, k5.
Work 2 more rows as established.

BEGIN KANGAROO CHARTS
Next row (RS) Work in established pat to 2nd marker, sm; joining separate balls of A and B as necessary, work row 1 of kangaroo chart 1 to next marker, sm; with A, work in established pat to end.

Cont to foll kangaroo chart 1 in this manner to row 44.
Cont to work kangaroo chart 2 over center 80 sts until row 175 has been worked. Cut B.
Next row (WS) K5, p to last 5 sts removing all markers except for first and last markers, k5.

Gauges
20 sts and 31 rows to 4"/10cm over St st using larger needle.
21 sts and 31 rows to 4"/10 cm over baby pine tree chart using larger needle.
Take time to check gauges.

Yahoo Kangaroo

Next row (RS) K7, sm, work row 1 of baby pine tree chart over next 90 sts, k36, work row 1 of baby pine tree chart over next 72 sts, sm, k7.
Work 3 more rows in established pat.
Next row (RS) K7, sm, work next row of baby pine tree chart to marker, sm, k7.
Cont to foll chart in this way to row 20.

TOP BORDER
Change to smaller needles. Knit 8 rows.
Bind off all sts knitwise.

Pocket
With B, cast on 10 sts.
Row 1 (RS) Knit.
Row 2 (WS) P1, M1 p-st, p to last st, M1 p-st, p1—12 sts.
Row 3 (RS) K1, M1, k to last st, M1, k1—14 sts.
Rows 4 and 5 Rep rows 2 and 3—18 sts.

Row 6 [P1 tbl, p1] in first st, M1 p-st, p to last st, M1 p-st, [p1 tbl, p1] in last st—22 sts.
Row 7 K1, M1, k4, M1, k to last 5 sts, M1, k4, M1, k1—26 sts.
Rows 8 and 9 Rep rows 2 and 3—30 sts.
Row 10 Purl.
Row 11 K1, M1, k to last st, M1, k1—32 sts.
Row 12 Purl.
Rows 13–16 Rep rows 11 and 12 twice—36 sts.
Row 17 K1, M1, k to last st, M1, k1—38 sts.
Rows 18–20 Work 3 rows even.
Rows 21–28 Rep rows 17–20 twice—42 sts.
Row 29 K1, M1, k to end—43 sts.
Rows 30–41 Work 12 rows even.
Row 42 P1, p2tog tbl, p to last 3 sts, p2tog, p1—41 sts.
Rows 43–45 Work 3 rows even.
Row 46 P to last 3 sts, p2tog, p1—40 sts.
Work even for 8 rows.
Bind off all sts loosely.

Finishing
EMBROIDERY
With C, work stem st (see page 182) for outline of kangaroo.
Work French knot (see page 182) for eye.
Cut 10"/25.5cm piece of C and split 4 plies in half. Using 2-ply strand, work 3 eyelashes in stem st.

POCKET
With WS facing, fold top edge of pocket so approx 1"/2.5cm at center and ¼"/.5cm at ends are folded to WS.
Sew edge to WS.
Sew pocket to blanket as shown in photo.
Weave in ends.
Block to measurements. ∎

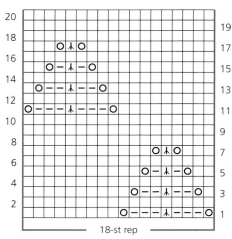

STITCH KEY

☐ k on RS, p on WS

⊟ p on RS, k on WS

O yo

人 S2PK

BABY PINE TREE CHART

18-st rep

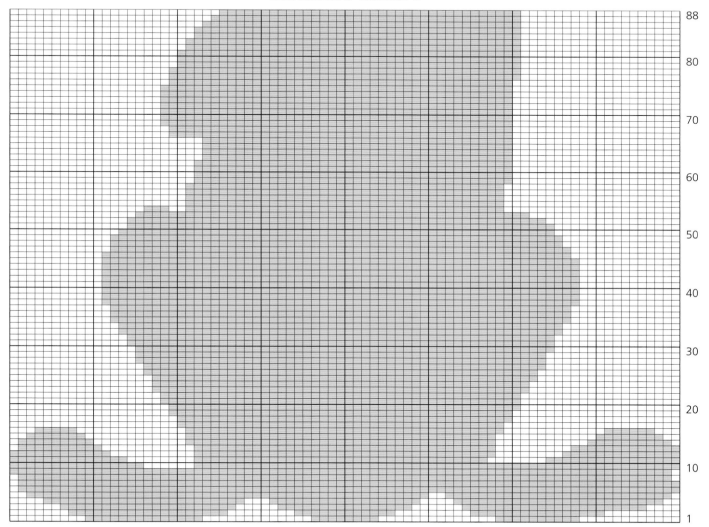

80 sts

Yahoo Kangaroo

KANGAROO CHART 2

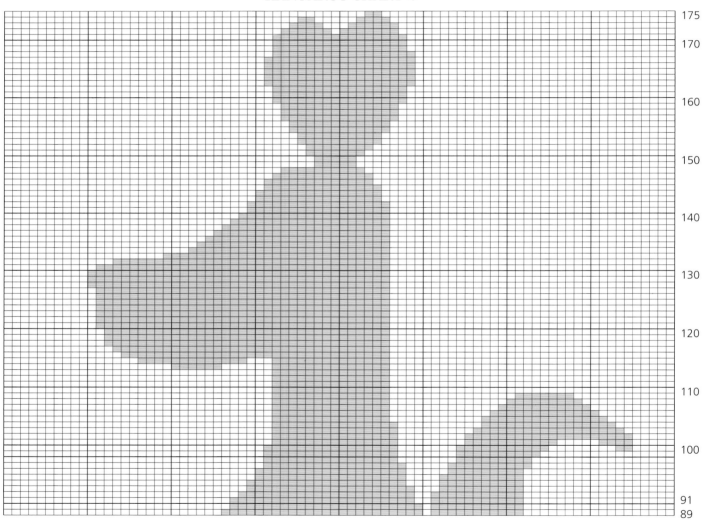

80 sts

COLOR KEY ☐ A ▨ B

Mer-baby Tail

Mermaid blankets are all the rage!
Now your favorite mer-baby can wiggle his or her fins while staying snuggly-warm.

DESIGNED BY JACOB SEIFERT

Sizes
Instructions are written for sizes 3 months (6–9 months, 12 months). Shown in size 3 months.

Knitted Measurements
Waist circumference Approx 24 (24½, 26)"/61 (62.5, 66)cm
Bottom circumference Approx 10 (11, 12)"/25.5 (28, 30.5)cm
Length (excluding fin) Approx 17 (21, 23)"/43 (53.5, 58.5)cm

Materials
- 2 (2, 3) 3½oz/100g balls (each approx 220yd/200m) of Cascade Yarns *220 Superwash* (superwash wool) in #1967 Wisteria (A) (3)
- 1 (2, 2) ball(s) in #840 Iris (B)
- One each sizes 6 and 7 (4 and 4.5mm) circular needles, 20"/50cm long, *or size to obtain gauges*
- One set (5) size 7 (4.5mm) double-pointed needles (dpn)
- Removable stitch markers
- Stitch holder

K1, P1 Rib
(over an even number of sts)
Rnd 1 *K1, p1; rep from * to end of rnd.
Rep rnd 1 for k1, p1 rib.

Seed Scale Pattern
(over an even number of sts)
Rnds 1 and 2 *Bring B to front, p1, bring B to back; with A, k1; rep from * around.
Rnds 3 and 4 *With A, k1; bring B to front, p1, bring B to back; rep from * around.
Rep rnds 1–4 for seed scale pat.

Seed St
(over an even number of sts)
Row 1 *K1, p1; rep from * to end.
Row 2 P the knit sts and k the purl sts.
Rep row 2 for seed st.

Double Seed Stitch
(over an even number of sts)
Row 1 (RS) *P1, k1; rep from * to end.
Row 2 (WS) *P1, k1; rep from * to end.
Row 3 *K1, p1; rep from * to end.
Row 4 *K1, p1; rep from * to end.
Rep rows 1–4 for double seed st.

Gauges
24 sts and 26 rnds to 4"/10cm over seed scale pat using larger needle.
26 sts and 26 rows to 4"/10cm over double seed st using larger needle.
Take time to check gauges.

Tail

RIBBED WAISTBAND

With A and smaller circular needle, cast on 72 (74, 78) sts, pm, cast on 72 (74, 78) sts—144 (148, 156) sts. Join, taking care to not twist sts, and pm for beg of rnd. Work in rnds of k1, p1 rib for 1 (1, 1½)"/2.5 (2.5, 4)cm.

BEGIN SEED SCALE PATTERN

Change to larger circular needle. Join B and work in seed scale pat for 3 (7, 8½)"/7.5 (18, 21.5)cm, end with a row 4.

TAIL SHAPING

Note Change to dpn when sts no longer fit comfortably on circular needle.
*Dec rnd 1 [With A, k2tog; *bring B to front, p1, bring B to back; with A, k1; rep from * to 2 sts before marker; bring B to front, p2tog tbl, bring B to back, sm] twice—4 sts dec'd.
Beg with rnd 4, work even in seed scale pat for 3 rnds more.
Dec rnd 2 [Bring B to front, p2tog tbl, bring B to back; *with A, k1; bring B to front, p1, bring B to back; rep from * to 2 sts before marker; with A, k2tog tbl, sm] twice—4 sts dec'd.
Beg with rnd 2, work even in seed scale pat for 3 rnds more.
Rep from * nine times more—64 (68, 76) sts.
Rep dec rnd 1 once more—60 (64, 72) sts.
Beg with rnd 4, work even in seed scale pat for 3 rnds more.

SEED STITCH FIN BASE

Cut B, cont with A only. Removing markers, sl first 30 (32, 36) sts to one dpn and next 30 (32, 36) sts to 2nd dpn. Hold dpn parallel and work onto larger circular needle as foll:
Next joining row (RS) *K first st on each needle tog; rep from * to end—30 (32, 36) sts. Place removable marker on this row

to indicate RS and cont to work back and forth in rows of seed st as foll:
Next inc row (WS) [Kfb] 5 times, *k1, p1; rep from * to last 5 sts, [kfb] 5 times—10 sts inc'd.
Rep last row once more—50 (52, 56) sts.
Next inc row (WS) [Kfb] 3 times, *k1, p1; rep from * to last 3 sts, [kfb] 3 times—56 (58, 62) sts.

DOUBLE SEED STITCH FIN

Work rows 1–4 of double seed st twice.

Fin shaping
Next dec row RS K2tog, *p1, k1; rep from * to end—1 st dec'd.
Next dec row K2tog, p1, *k1, p1; rep from * to end—1 st dec'd.
Rep last 2 rows 3 (4, 4) times more—48 (48, 52) sts.
Work rows 1–4 of double seed st twice.

Divide fin
Next row (RS) Cont in double seed st over first 24 (24, 26) sts, place rem 24 (24, 26) sts to holder.

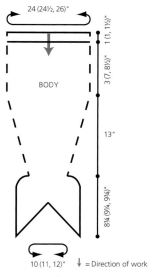

24 (24½, 26)"

1 (1, 1½)"

3 (7, 8½)"

BODY

13"

8¾ (9¼, 9¾)"

10 (11, 12)"   ↓ = Direction of work

Turn and work even in double seed st on first 24 (24, 26) sts for 5 rows.

First fin
Note Decreases are worked at end of RS rows.
Next dec row (RS) Work to last 2 sts, k2tog—23 (23, 25) sts.
Work even in double seed st for 5 rows.
Next dec row (RS) *Work to last 2 sts, k2tog—22 (22, 24) sts.
Work even in double seed st for 3 rows.
Cont in pat, dec 1 st at end of every RS row until 18 sts rem.
Next dec row Work to last 4 sts, p2tog, k2tog—16 sts.
Work WS row even in double seed st.
Next dec row Work to last 6 sts, k2tog, p2tog, k2tog—13 sts.
Work WS row even in double seed st.
Next dec row Work to last 7 sts, p1, k2tog, p2tog, k2tog—10 sts.
Work WS row even in double seed st.
Next dec row Work to last 6 sts, k2tog, p2tog, k2tog—7 sts.
Work WS row even in double seed st.
Next dec row Work in pat to last 6 sts, k2tog, p2tog, k2tog—4 sts.
Work WS row even in double seed st.
Next dec row Work 2 sts, k2tog—3 sts
Work WS row even in double seed st.
Next dec row P1, k2tog—2 sts.
Work WS row even in double seed st.
Next dec row K2tog.
Bind off last st.

Second fin
Turn work so WS is facing. Place removable marker to indicate this side is now RS. Join A at outer edge of 2nd half of fin. Cont in double seed st as established and work even on 24 (24, 26) sts for 4 rows. Work same as for first fin.

Finishing

Weave in ends. Block to measurements, pinning fin to desired shape. ■

Touch of Fair Isle

Just a touch of Fair Isle is all it takes
to turn a simple blanket into a spectacular one.

DESIGNED BY LARS RAINS

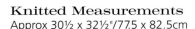

Knitted Measurements
Approx 30½ x 32½"/77.5 x 82.5cm

Materials
■ 4 3½oz/100g balls (each approx 220yd/200m) of Cascade Yarns *220 Superwash* (superwash wool) in #844 Periwinkle (A) ⬛3⬛
■ 1 ball each in #807 Raspberry (B), #820 Lemon (C), #821 Daffodil (D), and #877 Golden (E)
■ One size 6 (4mm) circular needle, 32"/80cm long, *or size to obtain gauge*
■ One size 7 (4.5mm) circular needle, 32"/80cm long
■ Stitch markers

Notes
1) Chart is worked using larger needle.
2) Circular needles are used to accommodate large number of stitches. Do *not* join.

Blanket
With smaller needle and A, cast on 169 sts. Knit 12 rows.
Row 1 (RS) K8, pm, k to last 8 sts, pm, k8.
Row 2 (WS) K8, sm, p to marker, sm, k8.
Row 3 K8, sm, k to last 8 sts, sm, k8.

Rep last 2 rows until piece measures approx 12½"/31.5cm from beg, end with a WS row. Cut A.

FIRST CHART BAND
Change to larger needle.
Row 1 (RS) With B, k8, sm; work 8-st rep of chart 19 times, work last st of chart, sm; with B, k8.

Cont chart in this way through row 13, with 8 sts at each end in garter st (k every row) and B. Cut yarns.

STOCKINETTE BAND
Change to smaller needle and join A.
Next row (WS) K8, sm, p to marker, sm, k8.
Next row (RS) Knit.
Rep last 2 rows seven times more. Cut A.

SECOND CHART BAND
Note For 2nd chart band, odd-numbered rows are WS rows (read from left to right), and even-numbered rows are RS rows (read from right to left).
Change to larger needle and work chart. Cut yarns.

Change to smaller needle and join A.
Next row (RS) K8, sm, p to marker, sm, k8.
Next row (WS) Knit.
Rep last 2 rows until piece measures approx 31¼"/79.5cm from beg, end with a WS row. Knit 12 rows, removing markers on first row. Bind off all sts loosely knitwise.

Finishing
Weave in ends.
Block to measurements. ■

Gauge
23 sts and 31 rows to 4"/10cm over St st using smaller needle.
Take time to check gauge.

49
Touch of Fair Isle

13

10

1

8-st rep

COLOR KEY

- B
- C
- D
- E

Heart to Heart

These charming heart motifs are knit individually
and then sewn together to form an adorable blanket for your little sweetheart.

DESIGNED BY UNJUNG YUN

Knitted Measurements
Approx 29 × 38"/73.5 x 96.5cm

Materials
■ 7 3½oz/100g balls (each approx 220yd/200m) of Cascade Yarns *220 Superwash* (superwash wool) in #820 Lemon (A) **3**
■ 1 ball in #229 Ash Rose (B)
■ One pair size 7 (4.5mm) needles, *or size to obtain gauges*
■ One size 6 (4.0mm) circular needle, 32"/80cm long
■ One size 7 (4.5mm) crochet hook
■ 30 removable stitch markers

Heart (Make 26 with A, 4 with B)
With larger needles, cast on 5 sts loosely.
Row 1 (RS) K1, yo, k3, yo, k1—7 sts. Mark this row as RS.
Row 2 K1, yo, k1 tbl, k3, k1 tbl, yo, k1—9 sts.
Row 3 K1, yo, k1 tbl, k5, k1 tbl, yo, k1—11 sts.
Row 4 K1, yo, k1 tbl, k7, k1 tbl, yo, k1—13 sts.
Row 5 K1, yo, k1 tbl, k9, k1 tbl, k1—14 sts.
Row 6 K1, yo, k11, k1 tbl, k1—15 sts.

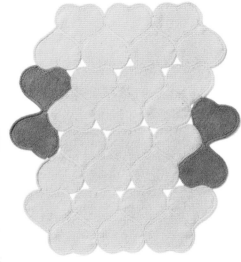

Row 7 K1, yo, k12, k1 tbl, k1—16 sts.
Row 8 K1, yo, k13, k1 tbl, yo, k1—18 sts.
Row 9 K1, k1 tbl, k14, k1 tbl, k1.
Row 10 K1, yo, k17—19 sts.
Row 11 K1, yo, k16, k1 tbl, k1—20 sts.
Row 12 K18, k1 tbl, yo, k1—21 sts.
Row 13 K1, k1 tbl, k19.
Row 14 K1, yo, k20—22 sts.
Row 15 K1, yo, k19, k1 tbl, k1—23 sts.

Row 16 K21, k1 tbl, k1.
Row 17 Knit.
Row 18 K1, yo, k22—24 sts.
Row 19 K1, yo, k21, k1 tbl, k1—25 sts.
Row 20 K23, k1 tbl, k1.
Row 21 Knit.
Row 22 K24, yo, k1—26 sts.
Row 23 K1, k1 tbl, k24.
Rows 24 and 25 Knit.
Row 26 K25, yo, k1—27 sts.
Row 27 K1, k1 tbl, k25.
Row 28 Knit.
Row 29 K1, yo, k26—28 sts.
Row 30 K1, ssk, k23, k1 tbl, k1—27 sts.
Row 31 Knit.
Row 32 K26, yo, k1—28 sts.
Row 33 K1, k1 tbl, k26.
Row 34 K1, ssk, k24, yo, k1—28 sts.
Row 35 K1, k1 tbl, k26.
Row 36 K27, yo, k1—29 sts.
Row 37 K1, yo, k1 tbl, k24, ssk, k1—29 sts.
Row 38 K27, k1 tbl, k1.
Row 39 K1, yo, k25, ssk, k1—29 sts.
Row 40 K27, k1 tbl, yo, k1—30 sts.
Row 41 K1, yo, k1 tbl, k25, ssk, k1—30 sts.
Row 42 K1, ssk, k25, k1 tbl, yo, k1—30 sts.
Row 43 K1, k2tog, k26, yo, k1—30 sts.
Row 44 K1, yo, k1 tbl, k25, k2tog, k1—30 sts.

Gauges
20 sts and 48 rows to 4"/10cm over garter st using larger needles.
Each heart measures approx 7¼ x 6¼"/18.5 x 16cm.
Take time to check gauges.

50

Heart to Heart

Row 45 K1, k2tog, k25, k1 tbl, k1—29 sts.
Row 46 K1, yo, k25, k2tog, k1—29 sts.
Row 47 K27, k1 tbl, k1.
Row 48 K1, yo, k25, k2tog, k1—29 sts.
Row 49 K1, k2tog, k24, k1 tbl, k1—28 sts.
Row 50 Knit.
Row 51 K1, k2tog, k24, yo, k1—28 sts.
Row 52 K1, k1 tbl, k26.
Row 53 K1, k2tog, k25—27 sts.
Row 54 Knit.

Row 55 K26, yo, k1—28 sts.
Row 56 K1, k1 tbl, k23, k2tog, k1—27 sts.
Rows 57 and 58 Knit.
Row 59 K1, k2tog, k24—26 sts.
Rows 60–62 Knit.
Row 63 K1, k2tog, k23—25 sts.
Rows 64 and 65 Knit.
Row 66 K22, k2tog, k1—24 sts.
Row 67 K21, ssk, k1—23 sts.
Rows 68 and 69 Knit.

Row 70 K20, k2tog, k1—22 sts.
Row 71 K19, ssk, k1—21 sts.
Row 72 Knit.
Row 73 K1, k2tog, k18—20 sts.
Row 74 K17, k2tog, k1—19 sts.
Row 75 K16, ssk, k1—18 sts.
Row 76 Knit.
Row 77 K1, k2tog, k12, ssk, k1—16 sts.
Row 78 K13, k2tog, k1—15 sts.
Row 79 K12, ssk, k1—14 sts.
Row 80 K11, k2tog, k1—13 sts.
Row 81 K1, k2tog, k7, ssk, k1—11 sts.
Row 82 K1, ssk, k5, k2tog, k1—9 sts.
Row 83 K1, k2tog, k3, ssk, k1—7 sts.
Next row (WS) Ssk, bind off loosely to last 2 sts, k2tog, pass 2nd st over first st and do *not* cut yarn. Leave st markers in place during assembly to indicate RS. With RS facing, insert crochet hook into last st, work 91 sl sts evenly around edge of heart, sl st in first sl st to join. Fasten off, leaving 10"/25cm tail for assembly.

Finishing

With RS facing and using photo as a guide, arrange hearts to form blanket. Sew hearts tog using whipstitch in back loops only.

EDGING
With RS facing, circular needle, B, and working along outer edge of one section of B hearts, pick up and k 1 st in each sl st.
Next row (WS) Knit.
Next row Purl.
Next row Knit.
Bind off knitwise.
Rep along rem B section.
With A, rep along outer edges of both A sections.
Weave in ends.
Block to measurements. ∎

51

All Tucked In

A trio of cheeky farm animals are tucked into bed; have fun knitting their cute little faces
—and their teeny toes, sticking out at the bottom of their "blanket"!

DESIGNED BY AMY BAHRT

Knitted Measurements
Approx 25½ x 32"/65 x 81cm

Materials
■ 3 3½oz/100g balls (each approx 220yd/200m) of Cascade Yarns *220 Superwash* (superwash wool) each in #824 Yellow (A) and #227 Bachelor Button (B) ⬛3⬛
■ 1 ball each in #817 Aran (C), #850 Lime Sherbet (D), #853 Butterscotch (E), and #1941 Salmon (F)
■ One pair size 7 (4.5mm) needles, *or size to obtain gauge*
■ One size 7 (4.5mm) circular needle, 32"/81cm long
■ One size G/6 (4mm) crochet hook
■ Brown sewing thread
■ Embroidery needle
■ Two white ½"/12mm 2-hole buttons
Note As small buttons are a choking hazard, embroider eyes if giving blanket to a child.
■ Polyester stuffing

Grid Stitch
(over a multiple of 7 sts plus 2)
Note Grid st pat begins on a WS row.

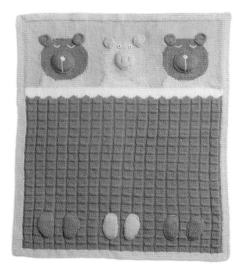

Row 1 (WS) *K2, p5; rep from *, end k2.
Row 2 (RS) *P2, k5; rep from *, end p2.
Row 3–6 Rep rows 1 and 2 twice more.
Row 7 Knit.
Row 8 Purl.
Rep rows 1–8 for grid st.

Notes
1) Circular needle is used to accommodate large number of stitches. Do *not* join.
2) Charts are worked in St st (k on RS, p on WS). When changing colors, twist yarns on WS to prevent holes in work.
3) When working charts 2 and 3, use separate ball of yarn for each color section. Do *not* carry yarn across back of work.

Blanket
With circular needle and A, cast on 138 sts.

BOTTOM BORDER
Knit 10 rows.

BEGIN GRID STITCH
Next row (RS) With A, k5 (border sts); join B, k128; join 2nd ball of A, k5 (border sts).
Next row (WS) With A, k5; with B, work row 1 of grid st across to last 5 sts; with A, k5.
Work even in pat as established until piece measures 22"/56cm from beg, end with a pat row 3 or 5.

BEGIN CHART 1
Row 1 (RS) With A, k5 border sts; work

Gauge
20 sts and 28 rows to 4"/10cm over St st using size 7 (4.5mm) needles
Take time to check gauge.

All Tucked In

8-st rep of chart 1 sixteen times; with A, k5 border sts.
Cont in pats as established, keeping 5 sts each side in garter st (k every row) with A and rem sts in chart pat, until 10 rows of chart 1 have been worked.

BEGIN CHARTS 2 AND 3
Row 1 (RS) With A, k5; join D and k10; join another ball of A and work row 1 of chart 2 over 30 sts; join another ball of D and k9; join another ball of A and work row 1 of chart 3 over 30 sts; join another ball of D and k9; join another ball of A and work row 1 of chart 2 across 30 sts; join another ball of D and k10; join another ball of A and k5.
Cont in pats as established until 46 rows of charts 2 and 3 have been worked.
Next row (RS) With A, k5; with D, k to last 5 sts; with A, k5.
Next row (WS) With A, k5; with D, p to last 5 sts; with A, k5.
Rep last 2 rows 8 times more.

TOP BORDER
With A only, knit 10 rows. Bind off.

Finishing
Weave in ends.
Block piece to measurements.

BEAR EARS (make 4)
With straight needles and E, cast on 5 sts.
Row 1 (WS) Purl.

Inc row 2 (RS) Kfb, k3, kfb—7 sts.
Row 3 Purl.
Inc row 4 Kfb, k5, kfb—9 sts.
Row 5 Purl.
Row 6 Knit.
Rows 7 and 8 Rep rows 5 and 6.
Dec row 9 Ssp, p5, p2tog tbl—7 sts.
Row 10 Knit.
Dec row 11 Ssp, p3, p2tog tbl—5 sts.
Dec row 12 Ssk, k1, k2tog—3 sts.
Bind off.
With E and embroidery needle, work chain st (see page 182) around entire ear

edge for clean finish.
Using chart 2 as a guide, sew cast-on rows of ears to bear heads.

BEAR NOSES (make 2)
With straight needles and E, cast on 6 sts.
Row 1 (WS) Purl.
Inc row 2 Kfb, k4, kfb—8 sts.
Inc row 3 Pfb, p6, pfb—10 sts.
Inc row 4 Kfb, k8, kfb—12 sts.
Row 5 Purl.
Inc row 6 Kfb, k10, kfb—14 sts.
Row 7 Purl.

CHART 1

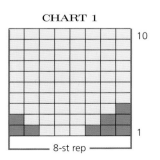

└── 8-st rep ──┘

CHART 2

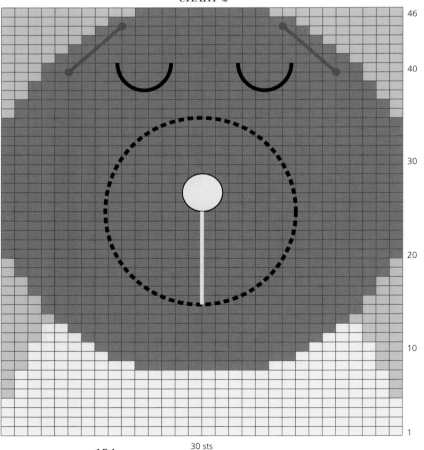

30 sts

Buffalo Borders

Combine classic buffalo-style plaid with a vibrant turquoise
and you've got an eye-catching border for baby's blanket.

DESIGNED BY ANN FAITH

Knitted Measurements
Approx 25 x 35"/63.5 x 89cm

Materials
▪ 4 3½oz/100g hanks (each approx
150yd/1375m) of Cascade Yarns *220
Superwash Aran* (superwash merino
wool) in #1998 Aqua (A) ◼4◻
▪ 1 hank each in #871 White (B) and
#1992 Deep Jungle (C)
▪ One size 8 (5mm) circular needle,
40"/100cm long, *or size to obtain gauge*

Notes
1) Carry yarn not in use loosely along
WS of work. Use separate balls of
contrast colors for each side when
working center section.
2) Circular needle is used to accommodate
large number of stitches. Do *not* join.

Blanket
With A, cast on 100 sts. Work 8 rows in
garter st (k every row).

BEGIN PLAID PATTERN
Rows 1 and 3 (RS) *With B, k4; with A,
k4; rep from * to last 4 sts; with B, k4.
Rows 2 and 4 *With B, p4; with A, p4;

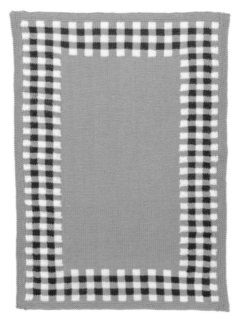

rep from * to last 4 sts; with B, p4.
Rows 5 and 7 *With A, k4; with C, k4;
rep from * to last 4 sts; with A, k4.
Rows 6 and 8 *With A, p4; with C, p4;
rep form * to last 4 sts; with A, p4.
Rows 9–16 Rep rows 1–8.

Rows 17–20 Rep rows 1–4.
Rows 21 and 23 [With A, k4; with C,
k4] twice; with A, k68; [with C, k4; with
A, k4] twice.
Rows 22 and 24 [With A, p4; with C,
p4] twice; with A, p68; [with C, p4; with
A, p4] twice.
Rows 25 and 27 [With B, k4; with A, k4]
twice; with B, k4; with A, k60; with B,
k4; [with A, k4; with B, k4] twice.
Rows 26 and 28 [With B, p4; with A,
p4] twice; with B, p4; with A, p60; with
B, p4; [with A, p4; with B, p4] twice.
Rep rows 21–28 seventeen times more,
then rep rows 21–24 once more.
Rep rows 1–20.
With A, work 8 rows in garter st.
Bind off.

SIDE EDGING
With RS facing and A, pick up and k 151 sts
evenly along side edge.
Work 8 rows in garter st.
Bind off.
Rep for rem side edge.

Finishing
Weave in ends.
Block to measurements. ◼

Gauge
18 sts and 24 rows to 4"/10cm over St st using size 8 (5mm) needle.
Take time to check gauge.

Framed Stripes

Pick a palette of related colors, like the cool blues and ivory shown here, stripe it up, and then frame those stripes with a snazzy ribbed border.

DESIGNED BY CHERYL MURRAY

Knitted Measurements
Approx 28 x 35¼"/71 x 89.5cm

Materials
- 3 3½oz/100g hanks (each approx 150yd/137.5m) of Cascade Yarns *220 Superwash Aran* (superwash merino wool) in #248 Flint Stone (A) **(4)**
- 1 hank each in #817 Aran (B) and #897 Baby Denim (C)
- One pair size 10 (6mm) needles, *or size to obtain gauge*
- One size 10 (6mm) circular needle, 40"/100cm long
- Stitch markers

Blanket
With B, cast on 90 sts.

BEGIN STRIPE PATTERN
Work in St st (k on RS, p on WS) as follows: *[2 rows B, 4 rows A] 3 times, 2 rows B, 8 rows C; rep from *4 times more,

[2 rows B, 4 rows A] 3 times, then 2 rows B. Bind off all sts loosely with B.

BORDER
With RS facing, circular needle, and A, pick up and k 88 sts evenly along cast-on edge, pm, 106 sts evenly along side edge, pm, 88 sts evenly along bound-off edge, pm, and 106 sts evenly along rem side edge — 388 sts.
Join and pm for beg of rnd.
Rnd 1 *K1, p1; rep from * to end.
Rnd 2 *K1, M1, work in established rib to marker, M1, sm; rep from * 3 times more — 8 sts inc'd.
Rep rnds 1 and 2 until ribbing measures approx 3"/7.5cm, working inc sts into pat. Bind off all sts loosely in rib.

Finishing
Weave in ends.
Block to measurements. ■

Gauge
16 sts and 22 rows to 4"/10cm over St st using size 10 (6mm) needles.
Take time to check gauge.

55

Bright Spot

Bright shades of blue and green alternate in this Fair Isle pattern;
a two-color border finishes it off to perfection.

DESIGNED BY LOIS S. YOUNG

Knitted Measurements
Approx 23½ x 26½"/59.5 x 67.5cm

Materials
■ 1 3½oz/100g ball (each approx 220yd/200m) of Cascade Yarns *220 Superwash* (superwash wool) each in #1919 Turtle (A), #886 Citron (B), #252 Celestial (C), and #849 Dark Aqua (D) ■
■ One size 6 (4mm) circular needle, 36"/90cm long, *or size to obtain gauge*
■ Stitch markers

Notes
1) Fair Isle pattern consists of three rows worked with colors A and B, followed by three rows worked with C and D. At the end of rows 3 and 9, do *not* turn work; slide stitches to other end of needle and work with new set of colors.
2) Chart is worked in St st (k on RS, p on WS).
3) Wet block blanket before adding border. Steam border after attaching it.
4) Circular needle is used to accommodate large number of sts. Do *not* join.

Blanket
With A, cast on 117 sts.

Work chart until piece measures 25"/63.5cm from beg or 1½"/4cm shorter than desired length. End with row 3 of pat but do *not* push sts to other end of needle at end of last row. Cut B. Bind off all sts loosely in A.

BORDER
With A and RS facing, and beg at lower right corner, pick up and k 108 sts evenly along side edge, pm, pick up and k 117 sts evenly along top edge, pm, pick up

and k 108 sts evenly along rem side edge, pm, and pick up and k 117 sts evenly along bottom edge—450 sts. Join and pm to mark beg of rnd.
Rnd 1 Purl.
Change to D.
Rnd 2 Knit, inc 1 st on each side of each corner marker—458 sts.
Rnd 3 Purl.
Change to C.
Rnd 4 Knit, inc 1 st on each side of each corner marker—466 sts.
Rnd 5 Bind off all sts loosely purlwise.

Finishing
Weave in ends.
Block to measurements. ■

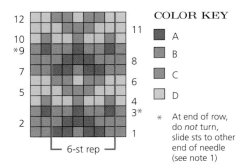

COLOR KEY
■ A
■ B
■ C
□ D

* At end of row, do *not* turn, slide sts to other end of needle (see note 1)

6-st rep

Gauge
21 sts and 23 rows to 4"/10cm over chart using size 6 (4mm) needle.
Take time to check gauge.

56

Covered in Cables

Cool stripes of blue and cream form the background
for beautifully intertwined cables in this stunning blanket.

DESIGNED BY KATHARINE HUNT

Knitted Measurements
Approx 25 x 34½"/63.5 x 87.5cm

Materials
■ 5 3½oz/100g hanks (each approx
150yd/137.5m) of Cascade Yarns *220
Superwash Aran* (superwash merino
wool) in #817 Aran (A) (4)
■ 3 hanks in #243 Dusty Blue (B)
■ One size 9 (5.5mm) circular needle,
40"/100cm long, *or size to obtain gauge*
■ Two additional size 9 (5.5mm) circular
needles for border
■ Cable needle (cn)
■ Stitch markers
■ Scrap yarn
■ One size I/9 (5.5mm) crochet hook

Stitch Glossary
3-st RC Sl 1 st to cn and hold to *back*,
k2, k1 from cn.
3-st LC Sl 2 sts to cn and hold to *front*,
k1, k2 from cn.
5-st RC Sl 3 sts to cn and hold to *back*,
k2, k3 from cn.
5-st LC Sl 2 sts to cn and hold to *front*,
k3, k2 from cn.

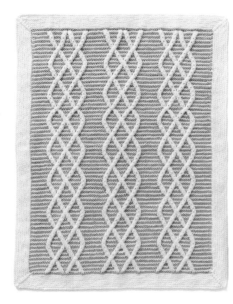

Notes
1) Circular needle is used to
accommodate large number of sts.
Do *not* join.
2) Cables are crossed on RS rows and
worked in A.

Blanket
With B, cast on 95 sts using the
provisional cast-on (see page 182).
Cast-on row counts as first knit row.
Inc row (WS) K16, *M1, k5, M1, k24;
rep from * once more, M1, k5, M1,
k16—101 sts.
Next row (RS) With A, knit.
Next row With A, *k8, p2, k7, p2, k1,
p2, k7, p2; rep from * 2 more times, k8.

BEGIN CHART PATTERN
Row 1 (RS) With B, *k8, pm, work row
1 of chart over 23 sts as foll: [sl 1 A st
wyib] twice, k7, [sl 1 A st wyib] twice, k1,
[sl 1 A st wyib] twice, k7, [sl 1 A st wyib]
twice, pm; rep from * twice more, k8.
Next row (WS) With B, *k8, sm, work
row 1 of chart over 23 sts as foll: [sl 1 A st
wyif] twice, k7, [sl 1 A st wyif] twice, k1, [sl
1 A st wyif] twice, k7, [sl 1 A st wyif] twice,
sm; rep from * twice more, k8.
Cont in pats as established, keeping 8 sts
between the chart pat in garter st (k every
row), alternating 2 rows A with 2 rows B,
and working chart through row 32.
Rep rows 1–32 six times more; then work

Gauge
16 sts and 34 rows to 4"/10cm over garter st using size 9 (5.5mm) needle.
Take time to check gauge.

Covered in Cables

rows 1–30 once more. Piece measures approx 31"/78.5cm from beg.
Next row (RS) With A, knit.
Next row (WS) With A, *k8, remove marker, p2, k7, p2, k1, p2, k7, p2, remove marker; rep from * twice more, k8.
Dec row (RS) With B, k15, *ssk, k5, k2tog, k22; rep from * once more, ssk, k5, k2tog, k15—95 sts.
Next row (WS) With B, knit. Cut B.

BORDER
With RS facing, long circular needles and A, remove provisional cast-on and place 95 sts on needle, pm, pick up and k 129 sts evenly along side edge, pm, k95 sts

from needle, pm, and pick up and k 129 sts evenly along rem side edge—448 sts. Join and pm for beg of rnd.
Distribute sts evenly over 2 needles.
Next rnd *P to marker, sm, k1, p to 1 st before marker, k1, sm; rep from * once more.
Inc rnd *Yo, k to marker, yo, sm, k1, yo, k to 1 st before marker, yo, k1, sm; rep from * once more—8 sts inc'd.
Rep last 2 rnds 6 times more—504 sts.
Bind off sts purlwise, knitting corner sts.

Finishing
Weave in ends.
Block to measurements. ■

STITCH KEY

☐ k on RS, p on WS

⊟ p on RS, k on WS

☑ slip 1 A st wyib on RS, slip 1 A st wyif on WS

⧄ 3-st RC

⧄ 3-st LC

⧄ 5-st RC

⧄ 5-st LC

COLOR KEY

☐ A

▦ B

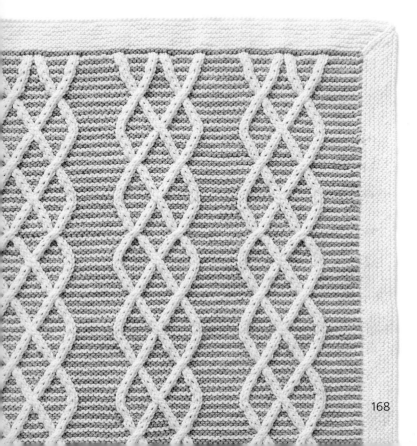

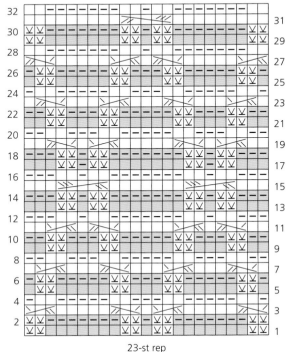

23-st rep

57

Triangle Tessellations

Brightly-colored triangles stack up in every direction
to create a modern geometric coverlet. Use bobbins to keep each color straight and have fun!

DESIGNED BY MATTHEW SCHRANK

Knitted Measurements
Approx 25 x 22½"/63.5 x 57cm

Materials
■ 2 3½oz/100g hanks (each approx 150yd/137.5m) of Cascade Yarns *220 Superwash Aran* (superwash merino wool) in #1992 Deep Jungle (A) **(4)**
■ 1 hank each in #242 Deep Sea Coral (B), #871 White (C), and #201 Sesame (D)
■ One size 8 (5mm) circular needle, 40"/100cm long, *or size to obtain gauge*
■ Bobbins

Notes
1) Use a separate bobbin for each color section. Do *not* carry yarn across back of work. When changing colors, twist yarns on WS to prevent holes in work.
2) To reduce number of ends to weave in, use one bobbin for stacked triangles of the same color as follows:
- Yarns for upright triangles are positioned to start next triangle of same color.
- Yarns for upside down triangles must be carried to starting point of next triangle of same color, twisting every few stitches to catch floats.

3) Chart is worked in Stockinette stitch (k on RS, p on WS).
4) Circular needle is used to accommodate large number of stitches. Do *not* join.

Blanket
With C, cast on 6 sts; with D, cast on 1 st; with B, cast on 13 sts; with A, cast on 1 st; [with C, cast on 13 sts; with D, cast on 1 st; with B, cast on 13 sts; with A, cast on 1 st] 3 times —105 sts.

BEGIN CHART
Row 1 (RS) Work 28-st rep 3 times, work to end of chart.
Cont to work chart in this manner until 14 rows of chart have been worked 10 times. Do *not* bind off.

I-CORD BIND OFF AND EDGING
With A, cast on 2 sts to RH needle.
Sl next st on LH needle to RH needle, k1, pass slipped st over knit st, sl 3 sts back to LH needle, *k2, sl 1, k1, pass slipped st over, sl 3 sts back to LH needle; rep from * until all sts along top edge are bound off.

Work 1 row of unattached I-cord at corner (k3, sl 3 sts back to LH needle), then work applied I-cord evenly along next edge as foll: *k2, pick up 1 st from edge, k1, pass picked up st over knit st, sl 3 sts back to LH needle; rep from * around rem 3 edges of blanket, working 1 row of unattached I-cord at each corner. Bind off and sew edges of I-cord tog.

Finishing
Weave in ends.
Block to measurements. ■

Gauge
16 sts and 24 rows to 4"/10cm over St st using size 8 (5mm) needle.
Take time to check gauge.

Triangle Tessellations

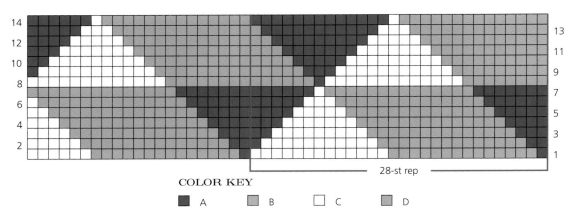

14		13
12		11
10		9
8		7
6		5
4		3
2		1

28-st rep

COLOR KEY

■ A ■ B □ C ■ D

170

58

Gingham Glory

This cheery checkered pattern is double-knit,
creating a reversible and super-toasty blanket to cuddle with.

DESIGNED BY DIANE ZANGL

Knitted Measurements
Approx 24 x 24"/61 x 61cm

Materials
- 2 3½oz/100g balls (each approx 220yd/200m) of Cascade Yarns *220 Superwash* (superwash wool) in #871 White (A)
- 2 3½oz/100g hanks (each approx 220yd/200m) of Cascade Yarns *220 Superwash Effects* (superwash wool) in #08 Pinks (B)
- One size 7 (4.5mm) circular needle, 24"/60cm long, *or size to obtain gauge*
- 18 stitch markers

Notes
1) Circular needle is used to accommodate large number of sts. Do *not* join.
2) Slip first st of every row purlwise wyif for selvage st.
3) Because blanket is reversible, there is no "right" or "wrong" side.
4) Borders are worked in garter st (k every row) with A, *not* in double knitting.
5) Short rows are worked over 6 garter st border sts on rows 11 and 12 to compensate for tighter row gauge of garter st.

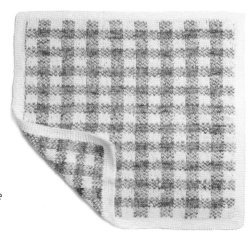

Gingham Pattern Notes
1) Gingham pat can be worked from written instructions or chart. Place marker every 10 sts (to show 5 st pairs) to make it easier to keep placement of blocks correct.
2) When knitting, *both* colors should be held at back; when purling, *both* colors should be held at front.
3) If working from chart, note that each square of chart represents 2 sts (one st pair). Knit first st in color shown, then purl next st in opposite color.

Even-numbered rows (side 1) are read from right to left; odd-numbered rows (side 2) are read from left to right.
4) Chart is not an accurate representation of finished blanket.
See photos for accurate representation.

Blanket
With A, cast on 97 sts.
Border row With A, sl 1 purlwise wyif (selvage st), k to end.
Rep border row 9 times more.
Inc row With A, sl 1 purlwise wyif, k5, pm, *k1 and p1 in next st; rep from * to last 6 sts, pm, k6—182 sts.
Mark next row as side 1.

BEGIN GINGHAM PATTERN
Row (side 1) With A, sl 1 purlwise wyif, k5, sm, *[k1 A, p1 B] 5 times, pm, [k1 B, p1 A, k1 A, p1 B] twice, k1 B, p1 A, pm; rep from * 7 times more, [k1 A, p1 B] 5 times, sm; with A, k6.
Row 2 (side 2) With A, sl 1 purlwise wyif, k5, sm, [k1 B, p1 A] 5 times, sm, *[k1 B, p1 A, k1 A, p1 B] twice, k1 B, p1 A, sm, [k1 B, p1 A] 5 times, sm; rep from * 7 times more; with A, k6.
Rows 3–6 Rep rows 1 and 2 twice more.

Gauge
15½ sts and 24 rows to 4"/10cm over gingham pat (measured on one side) using size 7 (4.5mm) needle.
Take time to check gauge.

Gingham Glory

Row 7 (side 1) With A, sl 1 purlwise wyif, k5, sm, *[k1 B, p1 A, k1 A, p1 B] twice, k1 B, p1 A, sm, [k1 B, p1 A] 5 times, sm; rep from * 7 times more, [k1 B, p1 A, k1 A, p1 B] twice, k1 B, p1 A, sm; with A, k6.

Row 8 (side 2) With A, sl 1 purlwise wyif, k5, sm, *[k1 B, p1 A, k1 A, p1 B] twice, k1 B, p1 A, sm, *[k1 A, p1 B] 5 times, sm, [k1 B, p1 A, k1 A, p1 B] twice,

k1 B, p1 A, sm; rep from * 7 times more; with A, k6.

Rows 9 and 10 Rep rows 7 and 8.

Short row 11 With A, sl 1 purlwise wyif, k5, turn, k6, turn; rep row 7.

Short row 12 With A, sl 1 purlwise wyif, k5, turn, k6, turn; rep row 8.

Keeping 6 sts each side in garter st with A for borders, rep rows 1–12 a total of 10 times, then rep rows 1–6 once more

(21 rows of blocks). Cut B.

Remove all markers except first and last.

Next row (side 1) With A, sl 1 purlwise wyif, k5, sm, *k1, p1; rep from * to marker, sm, k6.

Dec row Sl 1 purlwise wyif, k5, sm, *k2tog; rep from * to marker, sm, k6. Remove rem 2 markers.

Border row Sl 1 purlwise wyif, k to end.

Rep border row 8 times more.

Bind off loosely.

Finishing
Weave in ends.
Block to measurements. ∎

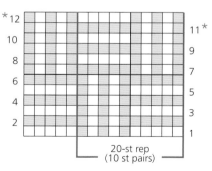

20-st rep
(10 st pairs)

COLOR KEY

☐ A

▨ B

* Short row, see written instructions

59
Mitered Crosses

A traditional quilting motif looks fabulous when translated into mitered squares.
It's join-as-you-go, so no pesky seams to sew!

DESIGNED BY KARIN FERNANDES

Knitted Measurements
Approx 27 x 33"/68.5 x 84cm

Materials
■ 5 3½oz/100g hanks (each approx 128yd/117m) of Cascade Yarns *128 Superwash* (superwash merino wool) in #871 White (A) ⑤
■ 2 hanks in #218 Opal (B)
■ One pair size 10 (6mm) needles, *or size to obtain gauges*
■ One size 10 (6mm) circular needle, 60"/150 cm long for I-cord edging
■ One size 10 (6mm) double-pointed needle (dpn) for I-cord edging
■ Stitch marker

Notes
1) Blanket is worked in mitered squares that are picked up and joined.
See diagram for guide.
2) Use backward loop cast-on throughout.

Blanket
SQUARE 1
With A, cast on 18 sts.
Row 1 (WS) K9, pm, k9.
Row 2 (RS) K to 2 sts before marker, k2tog, sm, ssk, k to end—2 sts dec'd.

Row 3 Knit.
Rep rows 2 and 3 six times more—4 sts.
Row 16 K2tog, remove marker, ssk, pass 2nd st over first st and off RH needle—1 st.
Do *not* cut yarn.

SQUARE 2
With A, RS facing, and rem st of previous square at top right of work, pick up and k 8 sts along top edge of previous square, cast on 9 sts—18 sts.
Rep rows 1–16 of square 1.

SQUARES 3–11
Work same as square 2.
Fasten off last st when square 11 is complete.

SQUARE 12
With A, cast on 9 sts.
With RS of square 1 facing, pick up and k 9 sts along right edge—18 sts.
Rep rows 1–16 of square 1.

SQUARE 13
With A, RS facing, and rem st of previous square at top right of previous square, pick up and k 8 sts along top edge of previous square, then 9 sts along right edge of neighboring square—18 sts.
Rep rows 1–16 of square 1, fastening off last st when row 16 is complete.

SQUARE 14
With B and RS facing, pick up and k 9 sts along top edge of previous square, then

Gauges
16 sts and 26 rows to 4"/10cm over garter st using size 10 (6mm) needles.
Each square measures approx 2½ x 2½"/6.5 x 6.5cm
Take time to check gauges.

9 sts along right edge of neighboring square—18 sts.
Rep rows 1–16 of square 1, fastening off last st when row 16 is complete.

SQUARES 15–22
Cont with colors in diagram, work same as square 13, fastening off last st when squares 19, 20, and 22 are complete.

Cont working squares in this way through square 143, using diagram as guide for colors, and fastening off rem st when foll square is in opposite color or at top of a column.

I-CORD EDGING
With circular needle, A, and RS facing, cont as foll: Beg at top right and working clockwise around blanket, pick up and k 1 st for each ridge and st along all edges. Cast on 3 sts to LH side of circular needle.
Row 1 With dpn, k2, ssk, sl 3 sts back to LH needle, then pull yarn tightly behind work. Rep row 1 to corner, then work three I-cord rows into corner st.
Cont working I-cord edging in this way along rem 3 edges.
Bind off and seam first and last rows of I-cord tog.

Finishing
Weave in ends. Block to measurements. ■

11	22	33	44	55	66	77	88	99	110	121	132	143
10	21	32	43	54	65	76	87	98	109	120	131	142
9	20	31	42	53	64	75	86	97	108	119	130	141
8	19	30	41	52	63	74	85	96	107	118	129	140
7	18	29	40	51	62	73	84	95	106	117	128	139
6	17	28	39	50	61	72	83	94	105	116	127	138
5	16	27	38	49	60	71	82	93	104	115	126	137
4	15	26	37	48	59	70	81	92	103	114	125	136
3	14	25	36	47	58	69	80	91	102	113	124	135
2	13	24	35	46	57	68	79	90	101	112	123	134
1	12	23	34	45	56	67	78	89	100	111	122	133

COLOR KEY
☐ A
▨ B

Bear Hug

Your little cub will get wrapped up in a big cuddly hug
created by this adorable bear-shaped snuggly!

DESIGNED BY AUDREY DRYSDALE

Knitted Measurements
Approx 34 x 26"/86.5 x 66cm

Materials
■ 5 3½oz/100g hanks (each
approx 150yd/137.5m) of Cascade
Yarns *220 Superwash Aran*
(superwash merino wool) in #200
Café Au Lait (A) **4**
■ 2 hanks each in #875 Feather
Grey (B) and #815 Black (C)
■ One size 8 (5mm) circular needle,
29"/74cm long, *or size to obtain gauge*
■ Stitch markers
■ One size 7 (4.5mm) crochet hook for
button loop
■ Tapestry needle
■ One ⅞"/22mm button

Double Seed Stitch
(over an odd number of sts)
Row 1 *K1, p1; rep from * to last st, k1.
Row 2 *P1, k1; rep from * to last st, p1.
Row 3 *P1, k1; rep from * to last st, p1.
Row 4 *K1, p1; rep from * to last st, k1.
Rep rows 1–4 for double seed st.

Stripe Pattern
Row 1 With B, knit.
Row 2 With B, purl.

Row 3 With C, knit.
Row 4 With C, purl.
Rep rows 1–4 for stripe pat.

Outer Layer
With A, cast on 3 sts.

BEGIN INCREASES
Row 1 (WS) Purl.
Row 2 [Kfb] twice, k1—5 sts.
Row 3 Pfb, p2, pfb, p1—7 sts.
Row 4 Kfb, k to last 2 sts, kfb, k1—2
sts inc'd.
Row 5 Pfb, p to last 2 sts, pfb, p1—2
sts inc'd.
Rep rows 4 and 5 until there are 155 sts,
end with a WS row.
Work even for 18 rows.

BEGIN DECREASES
Row 1 (RS) Ssk, k to last 2 sts,
k2tog—2 sts dec'd.
Row 2 P2tog, p to last 2 sts, p2tog
tbl—2 sts dec'd.
Rep rows 1 and 2 until there are 119 sts,
end with a WS row.

DIVIDE FOR LEGS
Next row (RS) Ssk, k54 (first leg); bind
off 7 sts; k to last 2 sts, k2tog (2nd

Gauge
24 sts and 40 rows to 4"/10cm over St st using size 8 (5mm) needle.
Take time to check gauge.

leg)—55 sts for each leg. Turn and work on 2nd leg only.

Next row (WS) P2tog, p to end of row—1 st dec'd.

Next row Ssk, k to last 2 sts, k2tog—2 sts dec'd.

Rep last 2 rows once more—49 sts.

Next row (WS) P2tog, p to end of row—1 st dec'd.

Next row K to last 2 sts, k2tog—1 st dec'd.

Rep last 2 rows until 29 sts rem.

Next row (WS) Purl.

Next row K to last 2 sts, k2tog—1 st dec'd.

Rep last 2 rows until 14 sts rem. Purl 1 row. Bind off.

Join A to 55 sts of first leg, ready to work a WS row.

Next row (WS) P to last 2 sts, p2tog—1 st dec'd.

Next row Ssk, k to last 2 sts, k2tog—2 sts dec'd.

Rep last 2 rows once more—49 sts.

Next row (WS) P to last 2 sts, p2tog—1 st dec'd.

Next row Ssk, k to end of row—1 st dec'd.

Rep last 2 rows until 29 sts rem.

Next row (WS) Purl.

Next row Ssk, k to end of row—1 st dec'd.

Rep last 2 rows until 14 sts rem. Purl 1 row. Bind off.

Eye Diagram

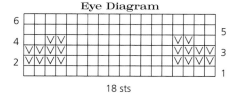

18 sts

STITCH KEY

Ⅴ duplicate st with C

Inner Striped Layer

With C, cast on 3 sts.

BEGIN INCREASES

Row 1 (WS) Purl.

Join B and begin striped pat, AT THE SAME TIME work same as for outer layer.

Leg Cover

With A, cast on 103 sts.

Work 2 rows of double seed st.

BEGIN INCREASES

Cont in double seed st, inc 1 st at beg and end of every RS row until there are 119 sts. Work even until piece measures 8½"/21.5cm from beg, end with a WS row. Place markers at each end of last row.

DIVIDE FOR LEGS

Next row (RS) Ssk, cont in pat over 54 sts (first leg); bind off 7 sts; work in pat to last 2 sts, k2tog (2nd leg)—55 sts each side. Turn and work on 2nd leg only.

Next row (WS) P2tog, work in pat to end of row—1 st dec'd.

Next row Ssk, work in pat to last 2 sts, k2tog—2 sts dec'd.

Rep last 2 rows once more—49 sts.

Next row (WS) P2tog, work in pat to end of row—1 st dec'd.

Next row Work in pat to last 2 sts, k2tog—1 st dec'd.

Rep last 2 rows until 29 sts rem.

Hood Diagram

Next row (WS) Work in pat.

Next row Work in pat to last 2 sts, k2tog—1 st dec'd.

Rep last 2 rows until 14 sts rem. Purl 1 row. Bind off.

Join A to 55 sts of first leg, ready to work a WS row.

Next row (WS) Work in pat to last 2 sts, p2tog—1 st dec'd.

Next row Ssk, work in pat to last 2 sts, k2tog—2 sts dec'd.

Rep last 2 rows once more—49 sts.

Next row (WS) Work in pat to last 2 sts, p2tog—1 st dec'd.

Next row Ssk, work in pat to end of row—1 st dec'd.

Rep last 2 rows until 29 sts rem.

Next row (WS) Work in pat.

Next row Ssk, work in pat to end of row—1 st dec'd.

Rep last 2 rows until 14 sts rem. Work in pat for 1 row. Bind off.

Hood

With A, cast on 3 sts and work as for outer layer until there are 91 sts, end with a WS row.

Work in double seed st for 6 rows, AT SAME TIME inc 1 st at beg and end of every row—103 sts. Bind off in pat.

Embellishments

EYES

With tapestry needle and C, work duplicate st eyes on RS of hood foll hood and eye diagrams.

NOSE

With C, cast on 3 sts.

Next row (RS) [Kfb] 3 times—6 sts.

Next row Knit.

Next row [Kfb] 5 times, k1—11 sts. Bind off. Wind the piece into a circle. With tapestry needle and C, sew circle closed. Foll hood diagram, sew nose to RS of hood.

OUTER EARS (make 2)

With A, cast on 10 sts.

Knit 1 row, purl 1 row.

Next row (RS) Kfb, k to last 2 sts, kfb, k1—12 sts.

Next row Purl.

Rep last 2 rows once—14 sts.

Work even for 6 rows.

Next row K1, k2tog, k8, ssk, k1—12 sts.

Purl 1 row.

Bind off.

INNER EARS (make 2)

With C, cast on 9 sts. Knit 1 row, purl 1 row. Join B and cont in striped pat as foll:

Next row (RS) Kfb, k to last 2 sts, kfb, k1—11 sts.

Next row Purl.

Rep last 2 rows once—13 sts.

Work even for 4 rows.

Next row K1, k2tog, k7, ssk, k1—11 sts.

Purl 1 row. Bind off.

With RS tog, sew inner ear to outer ear, then turn RS out. (Inner ear is slightly smaller than outer ear.)

Finishing

Place outer layer on table with RS facing up.
Place inner layer on top with WS facing up, matching edges of arms and legs.
Sew edges tog, leaving opening at top of head, and turn RS out.
Place wrap on table with outer layer RS up, then place hood on head with RS down.
Sew hood in place, working through all layers to close opening.
Turn hood to RS.
Foll diagram to sew ears in place along seam.
Place wrap on table with outer layer RS up, place leg cover on top with WS facing up, matching edges of legs.
Sew edges tog between markers; leave rest of piece unattached and turn RS out.

With crochet hook, sl st A to the end of the bear's right arm and ch for 1"/2.5cm, sl st to arm again forming loop.
Fasten off.
Sew button to RS of outer layer.
Weave in ends. ∎

Techniques

Kitchener Stitch

Cut a tail at least 4 times the length of the edge that will be grafted together and thread through a tapestry needle. Hold needles together with right sides showing, making sure each has the same number of live stitches, and work as follows:

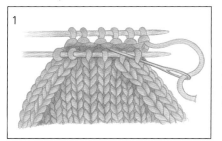
1

1) Insert tapestry needle purlwise through first stitch on front needle. Pull yarn through, leaving stitch on needle.

2

2) Insert tapestry needle knitwise through first stitch on back needle. Pull yarn through, leaving stitch on needle.

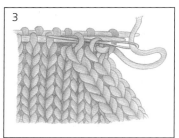
3

3) Insert tapestry needle knitwise through first stitch on front needle, pull yarn through, and slip stitch off needle. Then, insert tapestry needle purlwise through next stitch on front needle and pull yarn through, leaving this stitch on needle.

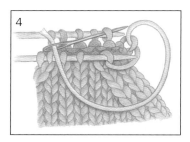
4

4) Insert tapestry needle purlwise through first stitch on back needle, pull yarn through, and slip stitch off needle. Then, insert tapestry needle knitwise through next stitch on back needle and pull yarn through, leaving this stitch on needle.

Repeat steps 3 and 4 until all stitches on both front and back needles have been grafted. Fasten off and weave in end.

Embroidery Stitches

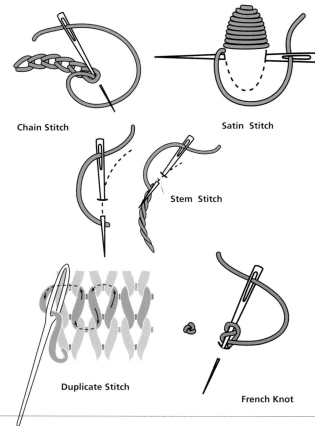

Chain Stitch

Satin Stitch

Stem Stitch

Duplicate Stitch

French Knot

Provisional Cast-On

With scrap yarn and crochet hook, chain the number of stitches to cast on, plus a few extra. Cut a tail and pull the tail through the last chain stitch. With knitting needle and yarn, pick up and knit the stated number of stitches through the "purl bumps" on the back of the chain. To remove scrap chain, when instructed, pull out the tail from the last crochet stitch. Gently and slowly pull on the tail to unravel the crochet stitches, carefully placing each released knit stitch on a needle.

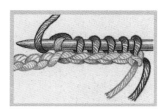

Things to Know

Abbreviations

approx	approximately	rep	repeat
beg	begin(ning)	RH	right-hand
CC	contrasting color	rnd(s)	round(s)
ch	chain	RS	right side(s)
cm	centimeter(s)	S2KP	slip 2 sts together,
cn	cable needle		knit 1, pass 2 slip
cont	continu(e)(ing)		stitches over knit 1
dc	double crochet	sc	single crochet
dec	decreas(e)(ing)	SKP	slip 1, knit 2, pass
dpn	double-pointed		slip stitch over
	needle(s)	SK2P	slip 1, knit 2
foll	follow(s)(ing)		together, pass slip
g	gram(s)		stitch over the knit 2
inc	increas(e)(ing)		together
k	knit	sl	slip
kfb	knit into the front and	sl st	slip stitch
	back of a stitch—	sm	slip marker
	one stitch is increased	ssk (ssp)	slip next 2 stitches
k2tog	knit 2 stitches		knitwise (purlwise)
	together		one at a time; knit
LH	left-hand		(purl) these 2
lp(s)	loop(s)		stitches together
m	meter(s)	sssk	slip next 3 stitches
M1	make 1 (knit st) by		knitwise, one at a
	inserting tip of LH		time, knit these 3
	needle from front to		stitches together
	back under strand between	st(s)	stitch(es)
	last stitch and next stitch;	St st	stockinette stitch
	knit into back loop	tbl	through back loop(s)
M1 p-st	make 1 (purl st) by working	tog	together
	same as M1 but purl	tr	treble crochet
	into back loop	WS	wrong side(s)
MC	main color	wyib	with yarn in back
mm	millimeter(s)	wyif	with yarn in front
oz	ounce(s)	yd	yard(s)
p	purl	yo	yarn over needle
p2tog	purl 2 stitches	*	repeat directions
	together		following * as many
pat(s)	pattern(s)		times as indicated
pfb	purl into front and back of a	[ ]	repeat directions
	stitch—one stitch is increased		inside brackets as
pm	place maker		many times as
psso	pass slip stitch(es) over		indicated
rem	remain(s)(ing)		

Skill Levels

■□□□
BEGINNER
Ideal first project.

■■□□
EASY
Basic stitches, minimal shaping and simple finishing.

■■■□
INTERMEDIATE
For knitters with some experience. More intricate stitches, shaping, and finishing.

■■■■
EXPERIENCED
For knitters able to work patterns with complicated shaping and finishing.

Knitting Needles

US	Metric
0	2mm
1	2.25mm
2	2.75mm
3	3.25mm
4	3.5mm
5	3.75mm
6	4mm
7	4.5mm
8	5mm
9	5.5mm
10	6mm
10½	6.5mm
11	8mm
13	9mm
15	10mm
17	12.75mm
19	15mm
35	19mm

Checking Your Gauge

Make a test swatch at least 4"/10cm square. If the number of stitches and rows does not correspond to the gauge given, you must change the needle size. An easy rule to follow is: To get fewer stitches to the inch/cm, use a larger needle; to get more stitches to the inch/cm, use a smaller needle. Continue to try different needle sizes until you get the same number of stitches and rows in the gauge.

index